THE WORLD'S GREATEST NATURAL AREAS:

An Indicative Inventory of Natural Sites of World Heritage Quality

D1515045

By

IUCN's Commission on National Parks and Protected Areas (CNPPA)

For

THE WORLD HERITAGE COMMITTEE

Commission on National Parks and Procted Areas

INTERNATIONAL UNION FOR CONSERVATION OF NATURE
AND NATURAL RESOURCES

1196 Gland, Switzerland

The presentation of the material in this document and the geographical designations employed do not imply the expression of any opinion whatsoever on the part of IUCN, Unesco, or the World Heritage Committee concerning the legal status of any country, territory, or area, or concerning the delimitation of its frontiers or boundaries.

Copyright International Union for Conservation of Nature and Natural Resources (IUCN)

Published with the financial support of the World Heritage Fund, and in cooperation with the United Nations Environment Programme.

Available from the Publications Department, IUCN, Avenue du Mont-Blanc, CH-1196 Gland, Switzerland.

ISBN: 2-88032-800-4

FOREWORD

Some places have special importance for people. They have inspired us by their beauty, given us insights into the history of life on our planet, taught us about the functions of natural ecosystems, informed us about the evolution of our own species and culture, enthralled us with wildlife spectacles, saved species of outstanding interest, and provided us with examples of how man can live in harmonious balance with his environment.

Many such places are so valuable that they form part of the heritage of all mankind.

As the 1960s drew to a close, people around the world became increasingly concerned that important parts of this natural and cultural heritage were in danger of being lost. Poor planning, poor management, and lack of the means to carry out conservation were the main reasons for this dangerous situation.

A new sense of urgency was felt at the international level. Just 10 years ago, in 1972, Unesco began its Man and the Biosphere Programme, the United Nations Environment Programme was started in Stockholm, and the 2nd International Conference on National Parks was held in Grand Teton. At each of these major events, the idea of a World Heritage Convention was discussed and promoted. Finally, in November 1972, the Convention for the Protection of the World Cultural and Natural Heritage was adopted by the Unesco General Conference, providing a framework for international cooperation in conserving the world's outstanding natural and cultural properties.

Under the Convention, a Committee of member governments is established to decide on sites which have been nominated for the World Heritage List. The Committee also provides technical assistance from the World Heritage Fund; at Nepal's Sagarmatha National Park, for example, the Fund is supporting solar power development to reduce the consumption of scarce firewood and help save the surrounding forests. Our most valuable resource is people, so the Fund also supports national training programmes and regional institutions such as the College of African Wildlife Management in Tanzania.

The Convention is unique because it deals with both cultural and natural properties. Certain archaeological sites or ancient buildings have an impact on history, art or science that transcends geographical boundaries; some townsites or groups of buildings are of special significance because of their architecture or place in the landscape; and some sites bear exceptional witness to a civilization which has disappeared. These outstanding works of man are an irreplaceable part of the world's cultural heritage.

Our natural heritage is an equally priceless legacy. Natural sites considered for the World Heritage List include areas which are of superlative natural beauty;

sites which illustrate significant geological processes; and natural habitats crucial to the survival of threatened plants and animals. These sites ensure the maintenance of the natural diversity upon which all mankind depends.

The "new" partnership between nature and culture given international recognition by the World Heritage Convention is not really new. It has just been forgotten in the modern rush to industrialize. For most of human history, people have lived as part of nature and even today all of us depend on nature for both its goods – such as forest products – and its services – such as watershed protection or recreation. The World Heritage Convention is a very useful means of reminding us of our link with nature. A number of sites already on the World Heritage List record man evolving with his environment. The Lower Valley of the Awash in Ethiopia has revealed the most complete skeleton of early pre-man yet known, and a whole family of early humans has been found, providing the earliest evidence of human social behaviour. From a nearby site on the Omo River come the earliest indications of human industry, in the form of stone tools. The use of tools gave man his dominant position in the Animal Kingdom.

At the Willandra Lakes site in Australia is recorded some of the earliest evidence of harvesting fresh-water animals and using grindstones to crush wild grass seeds to flour, showing man's evolving ability to harvest nature's goods.

Some of the earliest art was based on nature. At sites as far apart as the Vézere Valley in France and Kakadu National Park in Australia, there is evidence that art originated partly to give hunters a spiritual link with their prey, a link that survives among hunters to the present.

Some sites preserve villages where man flourished on the sustainable bounty of nature. The island known as "Skunggwai" to Canada's Haida Indians was so rich that these non-agricultural people had the leisure time to produce monumental wood-carving unmatched in the world. But not all early human use of the environment was sustainable. Mesa Verde National Park in Colorado, USA, records a long history of increasing human population and cultural sophistication. But suddenly, in the 13th century, settlements on the flat land were abandoned and villages were shifted to cliff caves; shortly after, Mesa Verde was abandoned, leaving behind a story of cultural complexity and, finally, failure.

From the very earliest periods, man has realized that variety is more than the spice of life: it is the very essence of life. Without the variety of geological formations, climates, and species that contribute to the diversity of ecosystems, without the distinctive contributions of every people, the whole immense tapestry of humanity would have quite a different pattern. The World Heritage Convention recognizes that if any part of our universal heritage is lost, mankind as a whole is the poorer.

Clearly, the Convention will work best if it is able to protect a significant portion of the world's outstanding natural and cultural sites. As part of IUCN's contribution to the Convention, the Commission on National Parks and Protected Areas (CNPPA) has prepared an indicative inventory of the world's most outstanding natural areas. This first international inventory of superlative natural sites is presented to illustrate the sorts of areas that might be considered of World Heritage quality; it is our hope that this list – far from exhaustive or complete – will stimulate additional ideas about outstanding sites for future editions of the inventory and, more immediately, encourage nominations of the listed sites and convince governments which have not joined the Convention to do so.

Nominating additional sites will provide increased protection for important areas and species and will illustrate the willingness of governments to undertake the responsibility of maintaining the integrity of their share of the World's Heritage. Clearly, a country does not need to be a Party to the Convention to be doing everything in its power to conserve sites of international importance. But joining the Convention helps to strengthen international solidarity in defence of the heritage of all mankind. By working together to achieve the objectives of the World Heritage Convention, all peoples and governments are contributing to a better future for humanity.

Jeffrey A. McNeely
Executive Officer
IUCN Commission on National Parks
and Protected Areas

2 September 1982
Gland, Switzerland

TABLE OF CONTENTS

THE WORLD'S GREATEST NATURAL AREAS:
An Indicative Inventory of Natural Sites of World Heritage Quality

By

IUCN's Commission on National Parks and Protected Areas (CNPPA)

INTRODUCTION

1. **The World Heritage Convention.** The Convention concerning the Protection of the World Cultural and Natural Heritage was adopted by the 1972 General Assembly of Unesco in recognition of the obligation of all nations to protect those outstanding natural and cultural areas which are of such unique value that they form a part of the heritage of all mankind. It provides a permanent legal, administrative, and financial framework designed to complement, aid and stimulate national programmes aimed at conserving this World Heritage.

By adopting the Convention, nations recognize that each country holds in trust for the rest of mankind those parts of the world heritage–both natural and cultural–that are found within its boundaries; that the international community has an obligation to support any nation in meeting this trust, if its own resources are insufficient; and that mankind must exercise the same sense of responsibility to the works of nature as to the works of its own hands. However, sovereignty of any World Heritage Site remains with the country where the site is located.

2. **The World Heritage Committee.** The Convention establishes both the "World Heritage Fund" and, as the instrument of cooperation in which all powers under the Convention are vested, an intergovernmental "World Heritage Committee". The Committee has three main functions:

– to identify, on the basis of nominations submitted by States Parties, cultural and natural properties of outstanding universal value which are to be protected under the Convention and to list these properties on the "World Heritage List";

– to decide which properties included on the World Heritage List are to be inscribed on the List of World Heritage in Danger (which can lead to emergency assistance);

– to determine in what way and under what conditions the resources in the World Heritage Fund (1981 technical assistance budget: US$1.2 million) can be used most advantageously to assist States Parties in the protection of their World Heritage properties.

3. **The role of IUCN/CNPPA.** IUCN, through its Commission on National Parks and Protected Areas (CNPPA), has been given responsibility under the Convention for advising Unesco on natural areas for inclusion on the World Heritage List. The Convention will best achieve its conservation objectives if it attracts more State Parties and if more natural properties are included on the list; therefore, IUCN/CNPPA are committed to stimulate both increased membership in the Convention and the addition of more natural properties to the World Heritage List.

4. **Criteria for including a natural property on the World Heritage List.** A natural property proposed for the List must meet at least one of the following four criteria (though meeting more than one criterion does not necessarily imply a more valuable site):

(i) be an outstanding example representing the major stages of the earth's evolutionary history (e.g., fossil beds, geological sites, ice-age landscapes);

(ii) be an outstanding example representing significant ongoing geological processes, biological evolution, and man's interaction with his natural environment (e.g., volcanoes, tropical rainforests, terraced agricultural landscapes);

(iii) contain superlative natural phenomena, formations, or features, or areas of exceptional natural beauty (e.g., superlative mountains or waterfalls, great concentrations of animals);

(iv) contain the foremost natural habitats where threatened species of animals or plants of outstanding universal value can survive.

5. **The relationship between World Heritage Sites and other categories of protected areas.** The primary objective of a World Heritage Site is to protect the natural features on the basis of which the area was considered to be of World Heritage quality. This is normally accomplished through existing national legislation and most World Heritage Sites will already have National Park or Strict Nature Reserve status. In some cases, reserved forest areas may be considered, but only when they are assured of perpetual protection. Some World Heritage Sites may also be Biosphere Reserves, but Biosphere Reserves are typically chosen for their representativeness of a given ecosystem type, while World Heritage Sites include only "areas of outstanding universal value". World Heritage status is meant to be exclusive, for only the very best areas; the Convention does **not** aim to protect all areas which are valuable or important.

6. **Background and Methods.** In May 1980, IUCN proposed to the Committee's Bureau that an inventory of natural sites be prepared. At the Fourth Session of the Committee, held in Paris in September 1980, the Committee "noted with satisfaction IUCN's plans for the preparation of a worldwide inventory of natural sites through worldwide distribution of questionnaires and organization of a series of expert meetings during the next two years". The first expert meeting to address the World Heritage Inventory was held in Garoua, Cameroon, in November 1980. The second inventory, covering the Neotropical Realm, was compiled on the basis of the working session of CNPPA held in Lima, Peru, in June 1981. The third, covering the Oceanian and Antarctic realms, was discussed at the CNPPA Working Session in Christchurch, New Zealand, in October 1981. And the fourth, covering the Nearctic, was developed on the basis of the CNPPA Working

Session in Waterton, Canada, in June 1982, after a detailed review process in the countries involved; however, not all of the North American sites listed on the indicative inventories of Canada and the USA are included here as this would have made the list longer than necessary for our purposes.

The Australian Realm is the only one that is entirely enclosed within the national borders of a single nation, greatly facilitating the survey and research that is required to suggest potential World Heritage Sites. In addition to five sites which have been elected to the List, or are currently under nomination, the additional sites listed in this inventory are those which have been proposed by the Australian Conservation Foundation, based on a lengthy process of national review. For the Palaearctic and Indomalayan Realms, the sites listed are based on information provided by IUCN contacts in the Realms, followed by a review process involving the relevant authorities in the relevant countries.

7. **Purposes**. The inventory is envisaged to have several uses:

– to assist countries in the preparation of the country inventories requested by the World Heritage Committee;

– to illustrate to countries the sorts of areas they have within their borders which may be worthy of World Heritage consideration–for countries who have not yet become Members of the Convention, this may help convince them to do so;

– to provide the World Heritage Committee with a list of outstanding areas to illustrate the potential number of sites to be considered, to facilitate comparisons between nominated sites, and to help redress the imbalance between natural and cultural sites;

– to stimulate the submission of nomination forms for the properties listed;

– and to provide guidance to the Committee for providing preparatory assistance to States Parties in need of such assistance.

8. **Limitations**. This inventory is a first edition and will be revised on a regular basis. It was compiled on the basis of suggestions made at the various working sessions of CNPPA, discussions with individuals knowledgeable about the countries involved, review by the CNPPA membership, and a literature search. It is not meant to be exhaustive or definitive, nor to replace national inventories; it is in no way binding on any government, nor does it imply any opinion whatsoever by the World Heritage Committee. As it is only indicative, further investigation may reveal that some sites do not meet the criteria stated in paragraph 5. In addition, there are certainly other sites not listed here which are of outstanding universal significance according to the criteria and which should be on the World Heritage List. It is expected that future editions of this inventory will reflect a growing knowledge of the world's natural heritage, so all comments and criticisms will be most welcome.

9. **The inventory**. The inventory is listed by biogeographic realm and by country, in alphabetical order, irrespective of whether the country is a State Party of the Convention (countries which are members appear in Appendix I); in cases where the property covers more than one country, it is listed under the first country. For each property, the name of the property is in capital letters, followed by a short statement of its universal significance and the criteria under which it qualifies for consideration for inclusion on the World Heritage List.

For sake of completeness, existing World Heritage Sites and properties which are currently being considered by the Committee are also included on the indicative inventory; existing World Heritage Sites are listed first under the relevant country. All sites are included on the schematic map covering the relevant biogeographic realm.

I. THE NEARCTIC REALM

1. **Name of property**: NAHANNI NATIONAL PARK (N.W. Territories) (elected WHS 1978)

   Country: Canada

   Universal significance: Nahanni is an area of 476,000 ha which includes outstanding physiographic, ecological, and geological features, providing an outstanding picture of the evolution of natural land features. Outstanding among these are examples of almost every distinct category of river or stream that is known; the finest examples of river canyons in Canada; the only one of North America's great waterfalls that has remained essentially undisturbed by man (Virginia Falls); the most spectacular karst terrain in the Western Hemisphere; and the spectacular sand blow-out known as "Devil's Kitchen", where the wind has eroded weird and fantastic pillars, knobs and arches.

   Criteria: (i), (ii), (iii)

2. **Name of property**: DINOSAUR PROVINCIAL PARK (Alberta) (elected WHS 1979)

   Country: Canada

   Universal significance: This 6,000 ha site includes the world's best representation of dinosaurs from the Upper Cretaceous period, yielding specimens from 60 species representing seven families of dinosaurs. In addition to the unmatched fossil riches, the site also has interesting riverine habitats, and significant populations of a number of rare and endangered species of plants and animals. The badland terrain which includes mesas, buttes, knife-edged divides, and many geological formations is of outstanding scenic value as well.

   Criteria: (i), (ii)

3. **Name of property**: BURGESS SHALE SITE (British Colombia) (elected WHS 1980)

   Country: Canada

   Universal significance: The World Heritage site is a relatively small area included within Yoho National Park, being composed of a quarry about 30 m long and 3 m wide. Within this very small area have been found more than 150 species of fossils assigned to some 120 genera; the majority of these have been found only in the Burgess Shales. Most of the fossils are of soft-bodied marine forms, which lack hard parts (making fossilization of such forms extremely rare); this site therefore provides the best available glimpse of the soft-bodied marine forms that were appearing at a period some half a billion years ago, early in the history of multi-cellular animal life on earth.

   Criteria: (i), (ii)

4. **Name of property**: BANFF AND JASPER NATIONAL PARKS (Alberta)

   Country: Canada

   Universal significance: These two contiguous national parks in the Canadian Rockies total 1.75 million hectares. Established in 1885, Banff (664,000 ha) was Canada's first national park. Its alpine setting, with outstanding natural attractions such as Lake Louise, Mt. Temple, Peyto Lake, Bow Lake and its glaciers, has attracted visitors from around the world since the turn of the century. Jasper National Park was established in 1907. Its southern boundary is contiguous with Banff National Park. In its west side lies Mt. Robson Provincial Park with Mt. Robson (3954 m) the highest point in the Canadian Rockies. Among its most outstanding features are the Columbia Icefields, the Maligne Valley and Medicine Lake. The Snaring River and Snake Indian River areas north of the town of Jasper form the largest contiguous block of wilderness in the mountain national parks; waters from the Park drain into the Pacific, Arctic, and Atlantic Oceans. Among the wildlife of the parks are found

Lake Louise, Banff National Park, Canada. (Photo : Dolder, WWF)

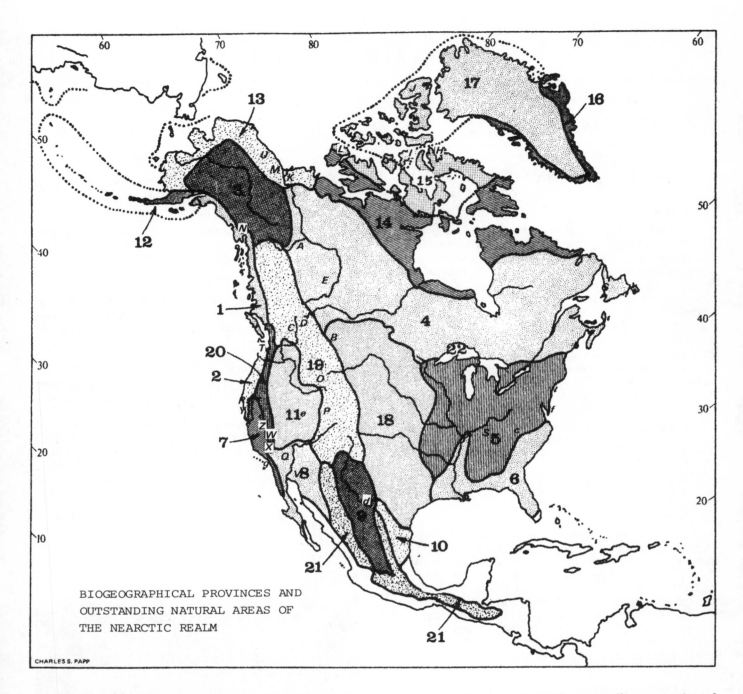

BIOGEOGRAPHICAL PROVINCES AND
OUTSTANDING NATURAL AREAS OF
THE NEARCTIC REALM

CHARLES S. PAPP

caribou, black and grizzly bears, mountain goats and sheep, and many others.

Criteria: (ii), (iii), (iv)

5. **Name of property**: WOOD BUFFALO NATIONAL PARK (Alberta/Northwest Territories)

Country: Canada

Universal significance: Wood Buffalo National Park encompasses an area of 4.3 million ha. Among its exceptional features of international importance is the Peace-Athabasca Delta, one of the largest freshwater deltas in the world. The Delta is the most northerly prairie marsh complex in North America and is a critical nesting and migratory habitat for countless waterfowl. The Park is perhaps most noted for its herd of 14,000 to 16,000 bison, the largest free-roaming herd in the world, and as the only known nesting area of the endangered whooping crane. The Park encompasses a

vast array of ecosystems and outstanding examples of ongoing aeolian, periglacial, semi-arid, fluvial and karst geomorphic processes.

Criteria: (ii), (iii), (iv)

6. **Name of property**: RODERICK HAIG-BROWN CONSERVATION AREA (British Colombia)

Country: Canada

Universal significance: The Adams River which runs through this site is one of the great salmon grounds in the world. Each year in excess of 1.5 million salmon return to the place of their birth more than 500 km up-river from the Pacific Ocean where they have spent the last two to three years of their short life. In an area of 65 ha is spawned a fishery worth millions of dollars per year. This two-week phenomenon attracts visitors from around the world.

Criteria: (iii)

MAP 1. OUTSTANDING NATURAL SITES OF THE NEARCTIC REALM

BIOGEOGRAPHICAL PROVINCES

1. Sitkan
2. Oregonian
3. Yukon Taiga
4. Canadian Taiga
5. Eastern Forest
6. Austroriparian
7. Californian
8. Sonoran
9. Chihuahuan
10. Tamaulipan
11. Great Basin
12. Aleutian Islands
13. Alaskan Tundra
14. Canadian Tundra
15. Arctic Archipelago
16. Greenland Tundra
17. Arctic Desert and Icecap
18. Grasslands
19. Rocky Mountains
20. Sierra-Cascade
21. Madrean-Cordilleran
22. Great Lakes

OUTSTANDING NATURAL SITES

A. Nahanni National Park
B. Dinosaur Provincial Park (Canada)
C. Burgess Shale Site (Canada)
D. Banff and Jasper National Parks (Canada)
E. Wood Buffalo National Park (Canada)
F. Roderick Haig-Brown Conservation Area (Canada)
G. Gros Morne National Park (Canada)
H. Eclipse Sound/Bylot Island (Canada)
I. Prince Leopold Island (Canada)
J. Ellesmere Island National Park (Canada)
K. Tuktoyaktuk Pingoes (Canada)
L. Thomsen River (Canada)
M. Beringian Refugium (Canada)
N. Kluane National Park/Wrangell St. Elias National Monument (Canada and USA)
O. Yellowstone National Park (USA)
P. Mesa Verde National Park (USA)
Q. Grand Canyon National Park (USA)
R. Redwood National Park (USA)
S. Mammoth Cave National Park (USA)
T. Olympic National Park (USA)
U. Arctic National Wildlife Refuge (USA)
V. Organ Pipe Cactus National Monument/Caneza Prieta National Wildlife Range (USA)
W. Death Valley National Monument (USA)
X. Joshua Tree National Monument (USA).
Y. Point Reyes National Seashore (USA).
Z. Sequoia/Kings Canyon National Parks (USA)
a. Yosemite National Park (USA)
b. Acadia National Park (USA)
c. Great Smoky Mountains National Park (USA)
d. Big Bend National Park (USA)
e. Bryce Canyon National Park (USA)
f. Virginia Coast Reserve (USA)
g. Grey Whale Lagoons of Baja California (Mexico)

---

7. **Name of property**: GROS MORNE NATIONAL PARK (Newfoundland)

   Country: Canada

   Universal significance: The scenic hills of Gros Morne National Park (194,250 ha) at the ocean's edge in western Newfoundland have been claimed by some geologists as "the Eight Wonders of the World". The rocks which form these hills represent ophiolites, relicts of the Earth's mantle and its overlying deep oceanic crust which were thrust up and over the ancient continental shelf of North America about half a billion years ago. Their emplacement was related to a collision of continents which formed the ancient Appalachian Mountain system. The history of that collision is nowhere better told than in the rocky cliffs of the park's coastline. In the past ten years increasing numbers of geologists have been attracted here to study various aspects of the timing and mechanisms of the collision process known as "plate tectonics".

   Criteria: (i), (ii)

8. **Name of property**: ECLIPSE SOUND/BYLOT ISLAND (Northwest Territories)

   Country: Canada

   Universal significance: Eclipse Sound/Bylot Island are in the eastern Arctic Ocean between Devon and Baffin Islands. The site is critical to the reproduction and survival of several million seabirds, and the bowhead whale, an endangered species, frequents the Sound in summer to feed. The Sound also supports approximately 10,000 Beluga whales and several thousand narwhal, the largest concentrations of these cetacean species in the world. Significant populations of seals and walrus inhabit the waters of the Sound as well, and its coastal reaches are a critical denning and summering area for the largest population in the world of the endangered polar bear.

   Criteria: (iii), (iv)

Yellowstone Falls, Yellowstone National Park, USA. (Photo: Franz Lipp, IUCN)

11

Grand Canyon National Park, USA. (Photo : Union Pacific Railroad, IUCN)

9. **Name of property**: PRINCE LEOPOLD ISLAND (Northwest Territories)

Country: Canada

Universal significance: Prince Leopold Island is located within Lancaster Sound off the northeast corner of Somerset Island, Franklin District, Northwest Territories. This flat-topped island with vertical cliffs 245-365 m high is a critical habitat for one of the largest seabird colonies in the circumpolar region of the world. There is a combination of high population densities of individual bird species and a high diversity of species present, a feature not found elsewhere in the Arctic. Preliminary 1975 breeding population numbers are: 140,000 thick-billed murres; 60,000 northern fulmars; 58,000 black-legged kittiwakes; 6,000 black guillemots and 4,000 glacucous gulls.

Criteria: (iii)

10. **Name of property**: ELLESMERE ISLAND NATIONAL PARK (Northwest Territories)

Country: Canada

Universal significance: An area of 39,500 sq km in the most northerly lands in Canada was reserved as a national park in 1982. The area includes the highest peaks in the Arctic as well as the only permanent ice shelf. The Lake Hazen area is a unique Arctic phenomena with arid characteristics and exceptional ecosystems. Fauna include musk-ox, caribou, arctic fox, and grey whales.

Criteria: (iii), (iv)

11. **Name of property**: TUKTOYAKTUK PINGOES (Northwest Territories)

Country: Canada

Universal significance: The Tuktoyaktuk Pingoes are situated in the Tuktoyaktuk Peninsula of the MacKenzie River Delta region of the Northwest Territories. This area contains the largest concentration of pingoes (ice-cored hills) in the world (1,400-1,500) and is an outstanding example of on-going geological processes associated with permafrost conditions. Ibyuk Hill, the largest pingo in Canada and perhaps the world, measures 900 m in circumference at its base and rises 40 m above the surrounding tundra. The pingo is deeply fissured and is occupied at its summit by a small crater-like pond.

Criteria: (ii)

12. **Name of property**: THOMSEN RIVER (Northwest Territories)

Country: Canada

Universal significance: The Thomsen River area lies along the north coast of Banks Island on the Western Arctic Islands, Northwest Territories. The area is a superlative example of the high-Arctic ecosystem. Its scenery is exceptional, including bold sea coasts near Cape Vesey Hamilton, spectacular canyons east of Mercy Bay, austere desert-like badlands west of Castel Bay contrasting with the lush, gentle hills of the Thomsen and Muskox River valleys. These river valleys are the best muskox range in the world and support the largest remaining herd of this relic of the last Ice Age (10,000-12,000 animals). The relationship between Inuit Indians and muskoxen in this area is also truly outstanding because it extends 3,400 years into the past and is one of the few instances in the world where a hunting economy developed based on Muskoxen as the staple resource.

Criteria: (ii), (iii), plus cultural criteria

13. **Name of property**: BERINGIAN REFUGIUM (Yukon)

Country: Canada

Universal significance: Located in the Yukon Territory, the area was not glaciated during the Illinoian and Wisconsin periods of glaciation when man was moving from Asia into North America, so the site is rich in archaeological and paleontological evidence of international importance. Wildlife is abundant. Dall sheep, moose and the famous Porcupine caribou herd cross the region; this is the only area in the world with 3 species of bears: polar bear, barren-ground grizzly and black bear. Bald eagles, osprey and peregrine falcon are also found.

Criteria: (i), (ii), (iii), (iv), plus cultural criteria

14. **Name of property**: KLUANE NATIONAL PARK/WRANGELL ST. ELIAS NATIONAL MONUMENT (elected WHS 1980) (Yukon and Alaska)

Country: Canada and USA

Universal significance: This site of over six and half million hectares is composed of protected areas in both Canada and the USA. It contains the largest non-polar ice field in the world and examples of some of the world's most spectacular glaciers; Icy Bay is the calving area for 3 major glaciers, producing a particularly scenic glacial landscape. The site contains a complete spectrum of glacial processes, from moraines and hanging valleys to cirques, keddles, and many others; the area is noted for its concentration of surging glaciers, including one which recently surged over 8 kms in two years. The large size of this site protects a number of complete watersheds of major rivers and shelters a large number of endangered species.

Criteria: (i), (ii), (iii), (iv)

15. **Name of property**: YELLOWSTONE NATIONAL PARK (Wyoming) (elected WHS 1978)

Country: USA

Universal significance: Yellowstone is the grandfather of all national parks. Its 900,000 ha include spectacular examples of the on-going geological processes of volcanism. These include the world's largest caldara (48 by 64 km), 27 fossil forests preserved by ash falls during volcanic eruptions, and the world's largest concentration of hot springs and geysers (most of the world's geysers are located within the park). The area is also of outstanding natural beauty, and the canyon of the Yellowstone has been called the "most beautiful canyon in the world". It also protects rare and endangered species such as grizzly bear, wolf, mountain lion, arctic grayling, yellowstone cut-throat trout, bald eagle and trumpeter swan.

Criteria: (i), (ii), (iii), (iv)

16. **Name of property**: MESA VERDE NATIONAL PARK (Colorado) (elected WHS 1978)

Country: USA *

Universal significance: Located in the forested table land at the edge of the San Juan range of the Rockies, Mesa Verde comprises just over 20,000 ha at the meeting place of mountain and desert. In the southern slopes are found a number of steep canyons, valleys, and mesa tops containing hundreds of pre-Colombian Indian villages. Some of these villages are in fact large towns with towers, terraces, and multiple level dwellings built of stone blocks in huge caves; one building, called the "Cliff Palace", has more than 200

Redwood National Park, USA. (Photo : Paul Dunckhørst, IUCN)

rooms. The surrounding national park preserves the sort of habitat that supported the Indians living in these villages over 500 years ago.

Criteria: (ii), (iii), plus cultural criteria

17. **Name of property**: GRAND CANYON NATIONAL PARK (Arizona) (elected WHS 1979)

Country: USA

Universal significance: Grand Canyon National Park, covering an area of nearly 500,000 ha, is widely believed to be the world's greatest geological spectacle, attracting millions of visitors each year to the 1500 m deep canyon; exposed in the canyon walls are rocks which have been deposited in each of the geological eras of the earth's history, one of the few places on earth where a person can literally walk through time. The geological features which have carved the valley have been continuing for over six million years and are still active today. The water action of the 70 major rapids and 400 lesser rapids within the park make the Colorado river the most challenging white water river in the United States. A number of endangered species also occur in the park. Finally, the Grand Canyon is also the site of important cultural resources, including over 2000 prehistoric Indian ruins.

Criteria: (i), (ii), (iii), (iv), plus cultural criteria

18. **Name of property**: REDWOOD NATIONAL PARK (California) (elected WHS 1980)

Country: USA

Universal significance: Redwood National Park covers nearly 37,000 ha and contains the tallest known living creatures on earth: the Redwood trees, *Sequoia sempervirens* (including one that is over 112 m tall). The Redwoods are surviving remnants of the group of trees that were once found throughout many of the moist temperate regions of the world. Now confined to just the wet coastal regions of west coastal North America, the Redwoods are under heavy commercial exploitation except in the few national parks and other protected areas where they occur.

Criteria: (ii), (iii), (iv)

19. **Name of property**: MAMMOTH CAVE NATIONAL PARK (Kentucky) (elected WHS 1981)

Country: USA

Universal significance: This 20,000 ha national park contains the longest cave system in the world, with its 306 km of known passages being over twice as long as the next longest cave system; scientists predict another 300 kms may yet be discovered. Nearly every type of cave formation is known within the site, and the geological processes are continuing. The flora and fauna of the cave system is the richest cave-dwelling wildlife known, with 12 of the 300 known species being rare and found only in Mammoth Cave.

Criteria: (i), (ii), (iv)

20. **Name of property**: OLYMPIC NATIONAL PARK (Washington) (elected WHS 1981)

Country: USA

Universal significance: The 360,000 ha contained within the Olympic National Park contain some of the most outstanding natural features in the world,

"The Hindu Temple" in Mammoth Cave National Park, USA. (Photo: US Dept. of the Interior, WWF)

including about 60 active glaciers, a spectacular wild coastline, and a coastal rainforest which may contain the highest living standing biomass (living matter) anywhere in the world; the world record individuals of Alaska cedar, grand fir, Pacific silver fir, western hemlock, Douglas fir, sub-alpine fir, and western red cedar are all found within the site. A number of endangered species of plants and animals thrive in Olympic. This site is also recognized as a Biosphere Reserve.

Criteria: (i), (ii), (iii), (iv)

21. **Name of property**: ARCTIC NATIONAL WILD-LIFE REFUGE (Alaska)

Country: USA

Universal significance: This area's varied topography, extending from the Brooks Range north to the Arctic Ocean, provides habitat for a tremendous diversity of wildlife, including caribou, polar and grizzly bears, musk ox, Dall sheep, Arctic peregrine falcons, and golden eagles. It is a virtually undisturbed arctic landscape, with coastal plain, tundra, valley, and mountain components. It is an outstanding example of biological evolution, superlative natural phenomena and areas of exceptional natural beauty.

Criteria: (ii), (iii)

22. **Name of property**: ORGAN PIPE CACTUS NATIONAL MONUMENT/CANEZA PRIETA NATIONAL WILDLIFE RANGE (Arizona)

Country: USA

Universal significance: This tract contains block-faulted mountains separated by wide alluvial valleys, along with playas, lava fields, and sands. It includes

Drake's Bay, Pt. Reyes National Seashore, USA. (Photo : US Dept. of the Interior, IUCN)

representative examples of the Sonoran Desert found in this region and nowhere else in the United States. Organ Pipe Cactus National Monument has been designated a Biosphere Reserve.

Criteria: (ii), (iii)

23. **Name of property**: DEATH VALLEY NATIONAL MONUMENT (California)

Country: USA

Universal significance: This large desert area, comprising over 800,000 ha, is nearly surrounded by high mountains, yet contains the lowest point in the Western Hemisphere. It is highly representative of Great Basin/Mohave Desert (mountain and desert) ecosystems.

Criteria: (ii), (iii)

24. **Name of property**: JOSHUA TREE NATIONAL MONUMENT (California)

Country: USA

Universal significance: This 223,000 ha area, located at the junction of the Mohave and Sonoran Deserts, contains an unusually rich variety of desert plants, including extensive stands of Joshua trees, set amongst striking granitic formations.

Criteria: (ii), (iii)

25. **Name of property**: POINT REYES NATIONAL SEASHORE (California)

Country: USA

Universal significance: The Point Reyes Peninsula, a unique living example of tectonic and seismic activity, has moved more than 500 km in the past 80 million years. A complex active rift zone, including the famed San Andreas Fault, occurs where the Peninsula meets the California mainland. The 26,000 ha area is characterized by a diverse set of habitats, striking scenery, and a large variety of animal species, including some of the largest concentrations of migratory shore birds found along the Pacific coast of North America.

Criteria: (ii), (iii), (iv)

26. **Name of property**: SEQUOIA/KINGS CANYON NATIONAL PARKS (California)

Country: USA

Universal significance: A combination of two adjoining national parks, this tract of nearly 340,000 ha includes Mount Whitney, the tallest mountain in the United States outside of Alaska, Mineral King Valley, and two enormous canyons of the Kings River. Groves of giant sequoia, the world's largest living things in terms of biomass, are found here; some of the trees are over 3,500 years old. Stretching over 100 kms from Kings Canyon in the north to Sequoia in the south, the two parks protect an unbroken wilderness of granite peaks, glacial lakes, gorges, flowering alpine meadows, and virgin forests of many different types. The site is also recognized as a Biosphere Reserve.

Criteria: (ii), (iii), (iv)

27. **Name of property**: YOSEMITE NATIONAL PARK (California)

Country: USA

Universal significance: Granite peaks and domes rise high above broad meadows in this 208,000 ha park in the heart of the Sierra Nevada, along with groves of sequoias and related tree species. Granite mountains, scenic lakes, glacier-carved valleys, and thunderous waterfalls, including the nation's highest (Yosemite

Falls, 800 m), are found here; El Capitan is the largest single block of granite in the world, with scarcely a fracture in its entire perpendicular wall. Five of the seven continental life zones are represented in Yosemite National Park.

Criteria: (i) (ii), (iii), (iv)

28. **Name of property**: ACADIA NATIONAL PARK (Maine)

Country: USA

Universal significance: Acadia, a 14,000 ha park situated on a rocky archipelago along the Maine coast, is an area of diverse geological features, dramatic topography (including the highest headlands along the entire Atlantic coast), and outstanding scenic beauty. It includes the finest surviving fragment of New England shoreline, virtually the only wild habitat in the entire region.

Criteria: (ii), (iii)

29. **Name of property**: GREAT SMOKY MOUNTAINS NATIONAL PARK (Tennessee/South Carolina)

Country: USA

Universal significance: This area of 208,000 ha includes one of the oldest uplands on earth, containing a diversity of lush vegetation associated with its varied topography, including spruce-fir, hemlock, deciduous, and mixed forests; some 1400 species of flowering plants are found in the site, along with about 2200 other plant species. About 70,000 ha of the site are virgin forest, the largest such block of these forest types in the USA. Fifty species of mammals occur, including an important roost of the Endangered Indiana Bat; the 200 species of birds include the Endangered Peregrine Falcon and Red-cockaded Woodpecker.

Criteria: (ii), (iii)

30. **Name of property**: BIG BEND NATIONAL PARK (Texas)

Country: USA

Universal significance: This 283,000 ha area contains excellent examples of mountain systems and deep canyons formed by a major river. A variety of unusual geological formations is found here, with many vegetation types – dry coniferous forest, woodland, chaparral, and desert – associated with them. The area has been designated a Biosphere Reserve. There may be possibilities of forming an international World Heritage Site with Mexico in this area.

Criteria: (ii), (iii)

31. **Name of property**: BRYCE CANYON NATIONAL PARK (Utah)

Country: USA

Universal significance: Bryce Canyon includes in its 14,500 ha innumerable highly colourful and bizarre pinnacles, walls and spires, perhaps the most colourful and unusual erosional forms in the world. Once part of a large inland sea into which sand, silt and lime was carried by rivers and streams from the surrounding highlands, the sediments began to shift as continental drift placed pressures on southern Utah; wind, snow, ice, frost, and rain began eroding the sediments into spires and pinnacles, with the softer shales and sandstones giving way first. The site has numerous trails which allow visitors to see the constantly changing scenery.

Criteria: (i), (ii), (iii)

32. **Name of property**: VIRGINIA COAST RESERVE (Virginia)

Country: USA

Universal significance: The Virginia Coast Reserve is the most well-preserved extensive barrier island system remaining on the Atlantic Coast of North America. The system of barrier islands, saltmarshes, and lagoons demonstrate dune and beach migration and storm action on barrier islands, and includes virtually all of the plant communities which once occurred along the Atlantic Coast. The area has been designated a Biosphere Reserve.

Criteria: (ii), (iii)

33. **Name of property**: GREY WHALE LAGOONS OF BAJA CALIFORNIA

Country: Mexico

Universal significance: This site covers several lagoons – Ojo de Liebre, Guerrero Negro, San Ignacio – and the Bahia de Magalena complex on the Pacific coast of Mexico, where the Endangered Grey Whales come to give birth. In the first two weeks of January, the area outside the lagoon entrance fills with whales migrating down from their inshore feeding grounds off the coast of Alaska; the females enter the lagoons to give birth, and by the first week in March, all calves have been produced and courting begins anew with spectacular chases and matings. By May, the whales have left their breeding grounds and returned north. While a few calves may be born in the open sea off the coast of California, the lagoons of Baja California provide their major breeding sites.

Criteria: (iv)

II. THE PALAEARCTIC REALM

1. **Name of property**: CHOUKOUTIEN (Hopeh Province)

Country: China

Universal significance: This is one of the richest fossil sites in the world. Notable among the many species which have been found at this site is *Homo erectus*, a widespread species of early man. There is some evidence at Choukoutien that this early form of man had already begun to use fire. Skeleton remains of over 30 males, females and children have already been recovered from this area. Research is continuing at Choukoutien.

Criteria: (ii), plus cultural criteria

2. **Name of property**: MOGAO GROTTOES (Kansu Province)

Country: China

Universal significance: Hewn in a steep cliff 10 km from Dunhuang is a honeycomb of caves, known as the Magao Grottoes, or the Caves of a Thousand Buddhas. Here man has used nature as an artistic medium of unsurpassed importance for Asian art. Brilliant paintings cover the cave walls and ceilings, each in its own artistic style, providing a complete and chronological picture of Buddhist art from the Eastern Jin (317 A.D.) to the Yuan Dynasty (1368 A.D.), nearly a thousand years of history. The 45,000 square metres of murals and 2,300 painted statues remain as bright as they were more than a thousand years ago. These paintings also depict social life in various historical periods and illustrate the friendly contact between China and other countries.

Criteria: (ii), plus cultural criteria

3. **Name of property**: CHANGBAISHAN NATURE RESERVE (Kirin Province)

Country: China

Universal significance: This 220,000 ha reserve contains deciduous broad leaf forest, mixed coniferous and deciduous broad leaf forest, sub-alpine coniferous forest, elfin woodland, and alpine tundra. The site contains a healthy population of the northeastern form of the tiger, plus plentiful prey species, such as sika deer. With the forest-covered volcanoes, crater lakes, waterfalls and hotsprings, this is an outstanding scenic reserve as well as an important habitat of endangered species of plants and animals.

Criteria: (i), (ii), (iii), (iv)

4. **Name of property**: GROTTOES OF KWEILIN (Kwangsi Chuang)

Country: China

Universal significance: The city of Kweilin is reputed to have China's most beautiful scenery. Located in karst country with a thick overlay of limestone, the city has many weird, isolated pinnacles that appear to have popped up from the ground, straight and high. The Grottoes of the city are particularly noteworthy, including such fascinating sights as the 3-metre-long rock dangling from a cave which contains two to three hundred statues of the Buddha (one of which is over 1,000 years old). The l-km chamber of the Seven Star Cave is a gallery of stalactites and stalagmites which have been given descriptive names such as "Monkey Picking Peaches", "Frog Leaping Into a Pond", "Two Dragons Entering a Cave", and "Two Dragons Playing Ball".

Criteria: (ii), (iii), plus cultural criteria

5. **Name of property**: MOUNT TAISHAN (Shantung Province)

Country: China

Universal significance: Rising 1,540 m above sea level, Mt. Taishan is a symbol of loftiness and grandeur. The rugged topography is covered in centuries-old pines and cypresses, magnificent temples and waterfalls. Beginning in the third century, emperors journeyed here to meditate, and scholars have left many poems and inscriptions praising the charm of the mountain. On a large flat rock in the Sutra Stone Valley, an ancient calligrapher has carved the text of the Buddhist Diamond Sutra, each character 50 cm high.

Criteria: (iii), plus cultural criteria

6. **Name of property**: WENCHUN WOLONG NATURE RESERVE (Sichuan Province)

Country: China

Universal significance: This 200,000 ha reserve is famous as the habitat of the endangered giant panda. The evergreen broadleaf forest, mixed deciduous and evergreen broadleaf forest, sub-alpine coniferous forest, alpine bush, and alpine meadow also provide habitat for other endangered species such as takin and golden monkey. Located on the boundary of the sub-tropical and temperate regions of China, this reserve contains a number of species from both zones, including several endemic species and economically valuable plants. This area was covered in ice during the Pleistocene epoch, so the landscape shows evidence of past glaciation. The site is a Biosphere Reserve.

Criteria: (iii), (iv)

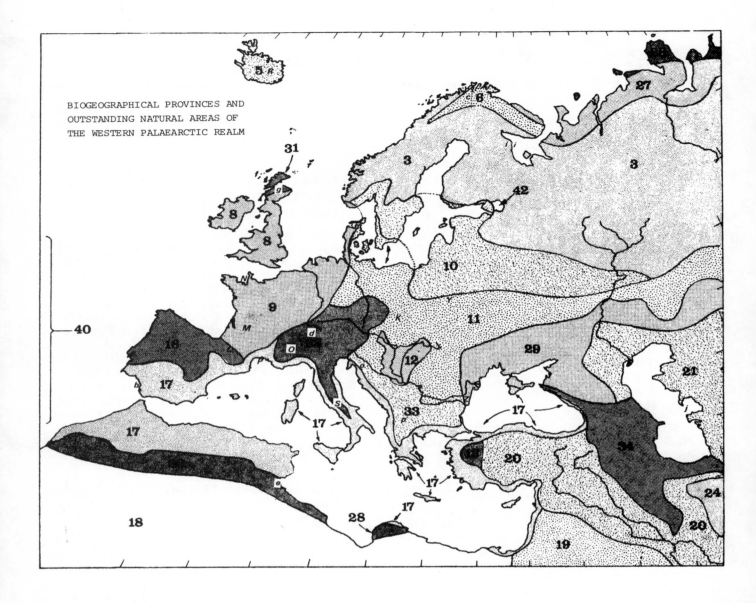

MAP 2. OUTSTANDING NATURAL AREAS OF THE PALAEARCTIC REALM

BIOGEOGRAPHICAL PROVINCES

1. Chinese Subtropical Forest
2. Japanese Evergreen Forest
3. West Eurasian Taiga
4. East Siberian Taiga
5. Icelandian
6. Subarctic birchwoods
7. Kamchatkan
8. British Islands
9. Atlantic
10. Boreonemoral
11. Middle European Forest
12. Pannonian
13. West Anatolian
14. Manchu-Japanese Mixed Forest
15. Oriental Deciduous Forest
16. Iberian Highlands
17. Mediterranean Sclerophyll
18. Sahara
19. Arabian Desert
20. Anatolian-Iranian Desert
21. Turanian
22. Takla-Makan-Gobi Desert
23. Tibetan
24. Iranian Desert
25. Arctic Desert
26. Higharctic Tundra
27. Lowarctic Tundra
28. Atlas Steppe
29. Pontian Steppe
30. Mongolian-Manchurian Steppe

OUTSTANDING NATURAL SITES

A. Choukoutien (China)
B. Mogad Grottoes (China)
C. Changbaishan Nature Reserve (China)
D. Grottoes of Kweilin (China)
E. Mount Taishan (China)
F. Wenchun Wolong Nature Reserve (China)
G. The Three Gorges of the Yangtze (China)
H. The Meridian Valleys (China)
I. The Turfan Basin (China)
J. Ice Forests of Mt. Qomolangma (China)
K. Pieniny National Park (Czechoslovakia and Poland)
L. Ras Muhammad (Egypt)
M. Decorated Grottos of the Vezere Valley (France)
N. Mont St. Michel and its Bay (France)
O. Grand Paradiso/Vanoise National Parks (France and Italy)
P. Camargue (France)
Q. The Pyrenees (France and Spain)
R. Skaftafell National Park (Iceland)
S. Abruzzo National Park (Italy)
T. Akan National Park (Japan)
U. Nikko National Park (Japan)
V. Fuji-Hakone-Izu National Park (Japan)
W. Nemegetu Basin (Mongolia)
X. Sagarmatha National Park (Nepal)
Y. Bialowieza National Park (Poland)
Z. Delta of the Danube Reserve (Romania)
a. Asir National Park (Saudi Arabia)
b. Coto Donana National Park (Spain)
c. Swedish Lapland (Sweden)
d. Bernese Oberland (Switzerland)

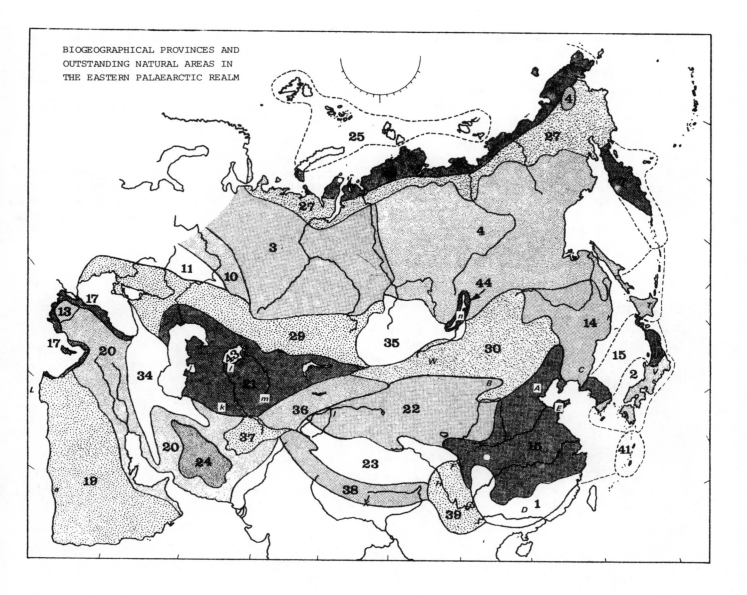

BIOGEOGRAPHICAL PROVINCES AND
OUTSTANDING NATURAL AREAS IN
THE EASTERN PALAEARCTIC REALM

31. Scottish Highlands
32. Central European Highlands
33. Balkan Highlands
34. Caucaso-Iranian Highlands
35. Altai Highlands
36. Pamir-Tian-Shan Highlands
37. Hindu Kush Highlands
38. Himalayan Highlands
39. Szechwan Highlands
40. Macaronesian Islands
41. Ryukyu Islands
42. Lake Ladoga
43. Aral Sea
44. Lake Baikal

e. Ichkeul National Park (Tunisia)
f. St. Kilda National Nature Reserve (United Kingdom)
g. Cairngorms National Nature Reserve (United Kingdom)
h. Sikhote-Alinsky State Reserve (USSR)
i. Kandalakcha State Reserve (USSR)
j. Kara-Bojaz Gol (USSR)
k. Badkhyzsky (USSR)
l. The Delta of the Amu Darya, on the Aral Sea (USSR)
m. Chatkalsky State Reserve (USSR)
n. Baikalsky and Darguzinsky State Reserves (USSR)
o. Plitvice Lakes National Park (Yugoslavia)
p. Lake Ohrid Region (Yugoslavia)

7. **Name of property**: THE THREE GORGES OF THE YANGTZE (Sichuan/Hupeh)

Country: China

Universal significance: The 6,300 km Yangtze River, the longest in China and one of the longest in the world, sweeps from west to east through eight provinces and one municipality; when it reaches the eastern Sichuan Basin in southwest China, it cuts through the Wushan Mountains bordering Sichuna and Hupeh provinces where the river course suddenly narrows and the waters become turbulent. Sheer cliffs and steep mountains rise on either side, creating one of nature's most fantastic sights: the Three Gorges of the Yangtze – the Qutang, the Wuxia, and Xiling – which extend a total of 193 kilometres from Fenjie in the west to Yichang in the east.

Criteria: (iii)

8. **Name of property**: THE MERIDIAN VALLEYS (Sichuan Province)

Country: China

Universal significance: This site contains an extraordinary geological formation, including deep valleys where three of Asia's largest rivers are found within a distance of 200 kms. The geological process of continental drift forced these rivers closer together as India collided with the Asian continent; the

Morsasjökull Glacier, Skaftafell National Park, Iceland. (Photo : WWF)

Yangtse, Mekong, and Selween rivers have survived this upheaval, forming deep channels through the new mountains. The mountains have provided an incredible laboratory for evolution of plants, with over 600 species of rhododrendrons having been described for the area.

Criteria: (i), (ii)

9. **Name of property**: THE TURFAN BASIN (Sinkiang Province)

Country: China

Universal significance: The 50,000 square kilometre Turfan Basin is set deep in the Tianshan Mountain Range, where it presents a changing panorama of deserts, gorges, sand dunes and wooded oases; in the centre of the depression is Aydingkol (Moonlight) Lake, 152 sq km in size and containing large amounts of crystalline salt, copper, and other minerals. Once an international trading centre and link in the cultural interflow between China and the West, Turfan is the site of many ancient tombs, Buddhist grotto art and ruins of ancient cities; 14 major cultural sites and relics are under government protection, among which is the ancient city of Gaochang, built at the beginning of the first century.

Criteria: (i), (ii), (iii), plus cultural criteria

10. **Name of property**: ICE FORESTS OF MT. QOMOLANGMA (Tibet Province)

Country: China

Universal significance: Mt. Qomolangma, known as Sagarmatha on its southern slopes in Nepal (where it is already a World Heritage Site), also has spectacular scenery on its Tibetan slopes. Most interesting are the ice forests, made up of tower-like ice and snow formations known scientifically as "seracs". They cover a vast area from 5,300 to 6,300 metres elevation, forming the world's most developed and best-preserved ice and snow structure. The ice towers assume fantastic shapes: majestic needles or sabres jutting into the sky; a seal resting on a pillar; a sitting giant panda to greet the visitor. These ice seracs are as clear as crystal and as sparkling as gems.

Criteria: (ii), (iii)

11. **Name of property**: PIENINY NATIONAL PARK

Country: Czechoslovakia and Poland

Universal significance: This 5,000 ha site is dominated by the Dunajec River, carving through steep narrow ravines and mighty precipices, surrounded by wooded slopes. The climate is uniquely warm for a site this far north, and the area was untouched by the glaciers of the Pleistocene epoch. The ancient mountains, well over 60 million years old, were incised by the Dunajec about 15 million years ago, forming a spectacular 9 km long valley. The mountains are entirely covered in lush and diverse deciduous forests of spruce, fir, larch, beech, elm, lime, maple, aspen, and ash, a result of the warm climate and favourable soil conditions; among the 1,100 vascular plants are several endemic and rare species. One hundred species of birds have been recorded, along with a rich mammalian fauna; particularly noteworthy are the bats, with 14 species recorded, an indication of the warm climate of the area.

Criteria: (iii), (iv)

12. **Name of property**: RAS MUHAMMAD

Country: Egypt

Universal significance: Located at the southern tip of the Sinai Peninsula, Ras Mahammad extends into the Red Sea, where a northern arm of Africa's great Rift Valley is submerged to a depth of over 2,000 metres. This subterranean depth traps sediment and silt where they are not agitated by currents, resulting in remarkably transparent waters. This is the site of some of the most spectacular coral reefs in the world, with the great depth providing unmatched diversity in marine life forms. Crocodile fish, moray eels, lion fish, a wide range of star fish and marine worms, and an amazing variety of corals make up what may be the world's most spectacular underwater landscape.

Criteria: (ii), (iii), (iv)

13. **Name of property**: DECORATED GROTTOES OF THE VEZERE VALLEY (elected WHS 1978)

Country: France

Universal significance: Over 100,000 years ago prehistoric man settled in the Vézere river valley, where they lived from hunting, fishing and gathering. In the past 100 years, chance discoveries and scientifically organized excavations have brought to light a rich harvest of remains from the rock shelters and caves where these people lived. Some 150 deposits studied so far have already yielded over 500,000 flint tools as well as fossil remains of the Cro-Magnon people who were living here. This area provides the world's best example of an extinct human culture which was living off nature's bounty. The caves are also of universal value in showing some of the world's earliest art work, including engraved (at Les Combarelles) and painted (at Lascaux and Fordde-Gaume), shedding new light on the origins of art, and clearly demonstrating that nature was the primary focus of the early artist.

Criteria: (ii), plus cultural criteria

14. **Name of property**: MONT ST. MICHEL AND ITS BAY (elected WHS 1979)

Country: France

Universal significance: In ancient times, this rocky islet off the Normandy coast was a Celtic place of worship. Then, in the 8th Century, an oratory dedicated to St. Michael, the archangel, was established, followed by an abbey. Later Gothic age constructions expanded the buildings, followed by a period of decline; then, during the past 100 years, restoration has brought splendour back to this monument, which is an outstanding example showing the balance between a geological site and human architecture.

Criteria: (iii), plus cultural criteria

15. **Name of property**: GRAND PARADISO/VANOISE NATIONAL PARKS

Country: France and Italy

Universal significance: This area of the Franco-Italian Alps covers over 200,000 ha of wild nature, including a number of peaks of over 3,000 metres including Grand Paradiso (4,061m) and Mont Blanc (4807m). This alpine area is excellent habitat for chamois and alpine ibex, with well over 10,000 chamois and perhaps as many as 5,000 ibex; the area

Mt. Fuji, Japan, from the shore of Shizu-Ura. (Photo: National Parks Association of Japan, IUCN)

provides an outstanding example of how endangered species can be brought back to significant population levels. While much of the area is fully protected, there is a very large buffer zone where shepherds and farmers continue to live in a traditional style.

Criteria: (ii), (iii), (iv), plus cultural criteria

16. **Name of property**: CAMARGUE

Country: France

Universal significance: This area of about 20,000 ha contains the Camargue Zoological and Botanical Reserve and several adjacent protected areas. A synthesis of natural and man-made wetlands, marshes, lagoons, meadows, and heath, this delta land is still in the process of creation, changing its appearance through the buildup of sediments carried from the Alps down to the Camargue by the Rhone river. With a combination of fresh, brackish, and salt water, this important wetland provides a very wide range of habitats, including eight main terrestrial biotopes. It is a very important habitat for birds, including 7 species which breed only here in France; the most spectacular of these is the flamingo. In addition, the area is an important winter habitat for migratory birds, with up to 200,000 ducks spending the cold months in the Camargue. While there are relatively few wild mammals, there are semi-wild cattle and white horses which provide a special attraction. The area is a Biosphere Reserve and holds the European Diploma.

Criteria: (ii), (iii)

17. **Name of property**: THE PYRENEES

Country: France and Spain

Universal significance: This site in the central Pyrenees includes approximately 20,000 ha, centred around the Valle de Ordesa National Park in Spain and several nature reserves in France. Located high in the Pyrenees, this spectacular area is a typical mountain glaciated landscape, with waterfalls, lakes, and glacier-carved valleys. It provides an important habitat for brown bear, as well as chamois, ibex and a number of other European species. Among the many species of birds are the lammergeier, grison vulture, and Egyptian vulture, and golden eagle. Vegetation extends from the deciduous forest at the lower levels, up to coniferous fir and pine forest and alpine meadows with rhododendrons and other typical alpine vegetation.

Criteria: (i), (ii), (iii) (iv)

18. **Name of property**: SKAFTAFELL NATIONAL PARK

Country: Iceland

Universal significance: This 500,000 ha area in Southeastern Iceland is a living glacial refugium, surrounded on three sides by Europe's largest glacier, but providing an excellent habitat where plants and animals live at the margin of an inland ice field. These conditions are similar to those that were typical in many parts of Europe during the last glacial period, the time when *Homo sapiens* was evolving into his present form. Over 200 species of flowering plants occur, including birch, willows, and a wide range of grasses and mosses. Being an oceanic island, Iceland has few species of native terrestrial mammals – only the Arctic fox – but the bird fauna is extremely rich, including skuas, gulls, and many others.

Criteria: (i), (ii)

19. **Name of property**: ABRUZZO NATIONAL PARK

Country: Italy

Universal significance: This 30,000 ha site is located in the central part of the Apennine mountain chain, dominated by three mountain peaks of over 2,000 metres in the southeastern portion of the park. The beech forests of the park are among the most magnificent in Europe, many of them over 500 years old. The area is notable for providing an important habitat for brown bear, with a population of about 100; chamois, with a population of about 300; and wolf with a population of 15-20. The first two have endemic subspecies within the park. Red deer, roe deer, and wild boar were reintroduced beginning in 1971, after having been exterminated by human activity.

Criteria: (iii), (iv)

20. **Name of property**: AKAN NATIONAL PARK (Hokkaido)

Country: Japan

Universal significance: This 87,000 ha site in eastern Hokkaido is a volcanic area in the sub-Arctic which contains a human population of about 15,000 Ainu, the aboriginal inhabitants of Japan. Two of the volcanoes, Me-Akan and Atosanupuri, are active. The area contains a number of scenic lakes, including the fantastically crystal-clear Lake Ashu, whose transparency of over 40 metres is considered the deepest water visibility in the world. Lake Okan has a unique freshwater plant, the marino or bol weed, a deep green algae, which forms velvety spherical structures 5 to 8 cm in diameter, growing at the bottom of the lake.

Criteria: (i), (ii), (iii), (iv) plus cultural criteria

21. **Name of property**: NIKKO NATIONAL PARK (Honshu)

Country: Japan

Universal significance: This area of 140,000 ha in northern Honshu is a harmonious blending of natural and artificial features, providing an ideal Japanese landscape. The most important cultural site is the Toshugu shrine dating from 1634-1636; it is surrounded by a vast area of mountains, lakes, and volcanoes, including four extinct volcanoes of over 2,000 metres elevation; a fifth volcano, Mt. Arsu, is still active. The landscape is still rapidly evolving, with an excellent system of lakes, swamps, and grassy plains which were lakes in the fairly recent past. Natural deciduous forests are found at lower elevations, giving way to Japanese species of conifers and finally alpine meadows. There is also an outstanding artificially planted cedar forest over 300 years old, leading up to the historical shrines at Toshugu. Mammal species in the site include the endangered Japanese serow, plus the Japanese black bear and Japanese macaque.

Criteria: (i), (iii), (iv), plus cultural criteria

Thyangbothe Monastery and Mt. Everest, Sagarmatha National Park, Nepal. (Photo: peter Jackson, WWF)

22. **Name of property**: FUJI-HAKONE-IZU NATIONAL PARK (Honshu)

Country: Japan

Universal significance: This complex of 4 protected areas totals over 120,000 ha and is dominated by one of the world's most famous mountains: Fuji Yama, an important feature in the religious, social, and artistic life of Japan. With magnificent forests, scenic lakes, hot springs, and lava flows, this is one of the world's most popular protected areas, with up to 15 million visitors per year.

Criteria:

23. **Name of property**: NEMEGETU BASIN

Country: Mongolia

Universal significance: This 100 km long site contains the most important dinosaur grave yards in Central Asia, yielding large numbers of a wide variety of dinosaur species; one expedition found nearly 120 tons of fossil bones. The bones were laid down during the Cretaceous period along a major river, surrounded by ponds and lakes and a broad delta some 40 km in width; this semi-aquatic habitat was an ideal environment for the support of a large population of dinosaurs.

Criteria: (i), (ii)

24. **Name of property**: SAGARMATHA NATIONAL PARK (elected WHS 1979)

Country: Nepal

Universal significance: This site of 124,000 ha encloses the southern slopes and approaches to the world's highest mountain, the 8848m Mt. Everest or

European bison in Bialowieza National Park, Poland. (Photo : Paul Garoudet, WWF)

Sagarmatha (as it is known to local residents). Other spectacular mountains are also included, including Nupste (7879m), Lhotse (8501 m), and Ama Dablam (6856m). Vegetation types vary from alpine scrub through colourful rhododendron forests into birch and silver fir forests. There is a representative selection of Himalayan fauna, including the endangered Snow Leopard and a number of species of pheasants; the yeti is said to be lurking in the wilder parts of the site. A number of villages of the Sherpa people are included in the site.

Criteria: (i), (ii), (iii), plus cultural criteria

25. **Name of property**: BIALOWIEZA NATIONAL PARK (elected WHS 1979)

Country: Poland

Universal significance: This site of just over 5,000 hectares is part of a much larger protected forest which stretches from Poland into the USSR. It is the last remaining example of Europe's primeval deciduous forest, providing a glimpse into the sort of habitat which once covered much of northern Europe, and in which European man evolved. The site is famous for being the last habitat of the European bison, a typical species of the European deciduous forest. Brought back from extinction and reintroduced into Bialowieza, it is now thriving, showing that man can save species and return them to productive levels. The site is a Biosphere Reserve.

Criteria: (iii), (iv)

26. **Name of property**: DELTA OF THE DANUBE RESERVE

Country: Romania

Universal significance: Comprising 40,000 ha on the Black Sea, the delta is a living landscape with a wide range of habitats and a collection of plants and animals containing a number of species found nowhere else in Europe. Habitats include rivers, brooks, channels, lakes, lagoons, marshes, swamps, reed beds, dunes, sandy plains, moorlands, grassy steppes, seasonally inundated islands, and permanently dry islands, but the major habitat is composed of reed beds which float on the surface. With such a wide range of habitats, the vegetation is unmatched in Europe, including seasonally inundated forests of a type found nowhere else on the Continent. Being located on the Black Sea, the climate is much milder than elsewhere in Europe, so the Delta is the winter habitat for a number of wintering geese, ducks and waders from northern Europe and Asia; notable among these is the red-breasted goose, with much of the world's population wintering in the Delta before breeding in the Siberian tundra during the summer. The vegetation varies from naked sandy beach to dense primeval forest, with the constantly changing conditions providing a mosaic of habitats. The area thus has a remarkably rich fauna, ranging from migratory waterfowl to permanently resident song birds in the many terrestrial habitats.

Criteria: (ii), (iii), (iv)

27. **Name of property**: ASIR NATIONAL PARK

Country: Saudi Arabia

Universal significance: This national park ranges from the rich coral reefs of the Red Sea up to the Saudi Arabian escarpment at an elevation of over 3000 m. This is by far the richest area in Saudi Arabia, with a very high rainfall in certain localities. The vegetation ranges from strand vegetation on the beaches through various deciduous and evergreen forest types up to montane scrub at the higher elevations. The fauna is probably the richest on the entire Arabian peninsula, including a number of species which are adapted to the lush vegetation conditions.

Criteria: (ii), (iii)

28. Name of property: COTO DONANA NATIONAL PARK

Country: Spain

Universal significance: This 7,000 ha area has been described by one expert as "the finest wilderness area still remaining in southern Europe and also the area richest in animals....the wealth of birds exceeds that of any other place in Europe". Located in the Delta of the Guadalquivir river, it is an almost untouched landscape with a great barrier of sand dunes separating the marshes from the sea. Vegetation varies from dunes to marshlands to savannas and woodlands, including important populations of cork oaks. The bird life is remarkable, including a number of migratory species which spend their winters in Coto Doñana, particularly the enormous flocks of ducks and greylag geese. The most important of the several endangered species found in the area is the Imperial eagle, the western race of which has its last stronghold in Coto Doñana.

Criteria: (iii), (iv)

29. Name of property: SWEDISH LAPLAND

Country: Sweden

Universal significance: This 843,000 ha wilderness north of the Arctic Circle, is the largest wild region of Europe, comprising 5 contiguous reserves: Padjelanta, Sarek, Stora Sjofallet, Sjaunja, and Tjuolta-Vuomde. The site includes all of Lapland's habitats and contains most species of plants and animals found in the northern coniferous belt of Europe. The glacial landscape is characterized by deep valleys, alpine plains, large glaciers, scenic waterfalls, peat bogs, swamp forests, and birch forests. The fauna includes all of the northern Europe species: linx, bear, wolf, wolverine, otter, moose (also called elk), domestic reindeer, and many others.

Criteria: (i), (ii), (iii), plus cultural criteria

30. Name of property: BERNESE OBERLAND

Country: Switzerland

Universal significance: This site contains the most spectacular landscape of the Swiss Alps, with spectacular mountains including Jungfrau (4158m), Eiger (3970m), Gross Fiescherhorn (4049m), Finsteraarhorn (4274m), Schreckhorn (4078m), and Wetterhorn (3701m). The mountain scenery is superb, with a full range of glaciers, snowfields, hanging valleys, meadow, and waterfalls (most scenic is Trummelback Falls). The area is dotted with small traditional villages and shepherd's huts, and criss-crossed by trails, chair-lifts, and Europe's highest (and most spectacular) railroad.

Criteria: (i), (ii), plus cultural criteria

Heron colony at Coto Donana, Spain. (Photo : C.A. Vaucher, WWF)

31. **Name of property**: ICHKEUL NATIONAL PARK (elected WHS 1979)

Country: Tunisia

Universal significance: This site is north Africa's most important wetland, providing an important habitat to hundreds of thousands of resident and migratory birds. From November to February, when most other north African wetlands are dry, Ichkeul provides an important habitat for vast numbers of birds which breed during the summer in Europe. These include 100,000 pochard and widgon, more than 180,000 coot, 9,000 greylag geese, 5,000 teal and shoveller, 2,000 pintail and tufted duck, and lesser numbers of a further 7 species of ducks. As the great lake at Ichkeul is at sea level, it is alternately freshwater and seawater, depending on the amount of rainfall that feeds the surrounding hills and rivers which drain into the lake. This ecological process makes the Ichkeul site extremely productive for fish, invertebrates, and aquatic plants, supporting the very significant populations of birds.

Criteria: (ii), (iii), (iv)

32. **Name of property**: ST. KILDA NATIONAL NATURE RESERVE

Country: United Kingdom

Universal significance: These islands, totalling 852 ha in area, are mountaintops emerging out of the Atlantic Ocean some 72 km west of the Outer Hebrides. The islands have probably been one of the Atlantic's greatest seabird colonies for tens of thousands of years. Among the most notable birds are the gannets, whose 45,000 pairs comprise about 57% of the world's total; puffins, fulmars, guillemots, kittiwakes, shearwaters, petrels, skuas and many species of gulls are also present. There is also one endemic species of mammal, the St. Kilda long-tailed field mouse, as well as soay sheep, which are now wild, but are based on an obscure domestic form. This site is a Biosphere Reserve.

Criteria: (iii), (iv)

33. **Name of property**: CAIRNGORMS NATIONAL NATURE RESERVE

Country: United Kingdom

Universal significance: This 26,000 ha site in Scotland's Grampian Mountains is a high barren expanse of granite mountains which has escaped the effects of man. Much of the reserve is covered in Caledonian forest, the type which covered much of the highlands but was mostly destroyed by the end of the 1700s. Of particular interest among the mammals is the small herd of reindeer which has been introduced from Sweden, bringing back a species which once occurred in Scotland, but was wiped out by human activities several hundred years ago. A number of species of birds rare in the UK occur in the reserve, including the Scottish crested tit, Scottish crossbill, snow bunting, ptarmigan, and many others.

Criteria: (iii), (iv)

34. **Name of property**: SIKHOTE-ALINSKY STATE RESERVE (Russian S.F.S.R.)

Country: USSR

Universal significance: This 31,000 ha site on the eastern flank of the Sikhote-Alinsky range on the coast of the Sea of Japan is a dissected mountainous area covered with broad leaved mixed forest at the lower elevations and various pine and spruce fir forest taking over higher up, to be replaced by mountain tundra at the highest elevations. A plant of particular interest in the reserve is ginseng. The site provides a mixture of Siberian and Chinese-Himalayan mammals, including wolf, Himalayan black bear, brown bear, sable, leopard, and Siberian tiger; in the coastal waters are Stellar's sealion, and harbour and ringed seal.

Criteria: (iii), (iv)

35. **Name of property**: KANDALAKCHA STATE RESERVE (R.S.F.S.R.)

Country: USSR

Universal significance: This 180,000 ha reserve comprises an archipelago of 53 islands in the Kandalakcha Bay of the White Sea, a number of islands in the Berents Sea, and the Lapland reserve on the Kola Peninsula; both tundra and taiga habitats are well represented. This desolate reserve is covered in low-growing vegetation, lakes, swamps, and peat bogs; seemingly devoid of life, there are in fact many species of mammals and birds, including moose, bears, wolverines and beavers. The birds are abundant in summer, and the area is a northern terminus for many migratory species.

Criteria: (ii), (iii)

36. **Name of property**: KARA-BOJAZ GOL (Turkmen SSR)

Country: USSR

Universal significance: This bay adjacent to the Caspian Sea is one of the world's most extraordinary phenomena. The 145 km wide bay lies about 3 metres below its parent sea, so water continuously rushes from the Caspian in what is widely considered to be the only salt water rapids in the world; the rapids are about 100 metres wide. Located in the desert of Turkmenistan, the Kara-Bojaz boils off water faster than the Caspian can supply it, providing one of the world's most saline bodies of water; the water's 35% mineral content is lethal to most forms of life, and the shoreline is covered in sodium sulphate as a result of the water's evaporation.

Criteria: (iii)

37. **Name of property**: BADKHYZSKY (Turkmen SSR)

Country: USSR

Universal significance: This 88,000 ha site at the southernmost tip of Turkmenistan is the best habitat for a wide range of desert fauna, including gazelles, wild goats, and some 1000 wild asses; the wild asses were nearly extinct when the reserve was established, but the population has now recovered to a productive level. Forty-eight mammal species have been reported including wild pigs, hyaenas, wolves, honey badgers and caracal. The vegetation is also of extreme interest, with broad savannas dotted with pastacio trees;

Loch an Eilan, Cairngorms National Nature Reserve, United Kingdom. (Photo : Robert M. Adam, WWF)

another unique plant is the ferula, which attains its full growth within 6 weeks in spring time then withers away for 6 to 9 years until it suddenly bursts into bloom, launching its seeds into the wind; having completed its life cycle, the plant then dies away. The area is also of outstanding geological interest, with the 500 metre-deep Er-Oylan-Duz depression stretching some 25 kms, with jet black mountains falling sharply to a gleeming white salt lake surrounded by grotesque jutting rock formations.

Criteria: (ii), (iii), (iv)

38. **Name of property**: THE DELTA OF THE AMU DARYA, ON THE ARAL SEA (Uzbek SSR)

Country: USSR

Universal significance: Once one of the largest rivers in Central Asia, the Amu Darya is still a major river which extends 2,500 km from the Hindu Kush to the Aral Sea. With two flood periods (one in spring from falling snow, the other later in summer from melting of mountain glaciers), the river carries twice as much alluvium as the Nile. The sediment load has helped to force the river to change its course, as it once flowed into the Caspian Sea. The Delta has unique riverine forests, known as "tugai", which are composed of dense reeds, trees and shrubs; this vegetation is often impenetrable, but it offers a useful habitat to a number of species of animals.

Criteria: (i), (ii)

39. **Name of property**: CHATKALSKY STATE RESERVE (Uzbek SSR)

Country: USSR

Universal significance: This 35,000 ha site comprises the three western spurs of the Chatkalsky range of the Tien Shan mountains east of Tashkent. Ranging from 1000-4000 m, these mountains of debonian, permian, carboniferous age are steep and deeply cut by precipitous valleys. Typical forest types are junipers (three species), and deciduous forests with reasonably diverse flora. The area provides an important habitat for the endangered snow leopard and contains other rare species such as the endemic menzbier's marmot and Siberian ibex.

Criteria: (i), iv)

40. **Name of property**: BAIKALSKY AND DARGU-ZINSKY STATE RESERVES (Russian S.F.S.R.)

Country: USSR

Universal significance: These sites together comprising some 430,000 ha include the world's deepest lake, Lake Baikal, and surrounding country. The mountainous section is almost inaccessible, being very deeply dissected, with numerous glacial cirques and lakes, the sources of mountain torrents. The climate is severe, with 210 days below freezing point per year. There is a wide range of forest types, taiga, tundra, and peaty meadows. The fauna is extremely rich including some 220 species of birds, and over 40 species of mammals; notable among these is the only freshwater seal in the world, the endemic Baikal hairseal, a local race of musk deer, the sable, and reindeer. Baikal is by far the oldest lake in the world, at least some 25 million years old; as a result of this great age some three quarters of the 1200 species of animals are endemic to the lake, including entire genera and even families. Baikal is the world's deepest lake, some 1.5 km deep and contains a fifth of the world's total freshwater reserves.

Criteria: (i), (ii), (iii), (iv)

41. **Name of property**: PLITVICE LAKES NATIONAL PARK (elected WHS 1978)

Country: Yugoslavia

Universal significance: The site is an outstanding example of natural architecture in movement. Weaving among limestone and dolomite rock formation, the Korona river in Queresha suddenly pauses to form a chain of some 20 lakes and emerald green pools. These lakes descend in steps separated by natural dams broached by waterfalls that are often over 20 metres high. This landscape of stone and water was built by living organisms; mosses, algae and bacteria have all been encrusted and fossilized by deposits of calcium carbonate. The cave-pitted natural dams between the lakes grow about 1 cm higher each year.

Criteria: (ii), (iii)

42. **Name of property**: LAKE OHRID REGION (elected WHS 1979)

Country: Yugoslavia

Universal significance: Lake Ohrid is one of the oldest lakes in the world. Its warm dark blue waters, transparent to a depth of at least 20 metres, are drawn from springs and contain living fossils, creatures which have scarcely changed since the Pleistocene era began, being isolated from other lake and river systems. Some of the lake's sponges are unique, and along with many species of snail and certain species of fish, they constitute an animal life which is considered to be one of the last remnants of the ancient aquatic region of the Eurasian continent before the Ice Ages. There are traces of human settlement along the lake which stretch back without a break to Neolithic times.

Criteria: (i), (ii), (iii), plus cultural criteria

III. THE AFROTROPICAL REALM

1. **Name of property**: TASSILI N'AJJER NATIONAL PARK (nominated WHS 1981)

   Country: Algeria

   Universal significance: The geological formations of this site are of outstanding scenic interest, with Pre-Cambrian crystalline formations and eroded sandstones forming "forests of rocks". The flora and fauna shows relationships to prehistoric periods when the Tassili region was considerably more moist; that humans knew such conditions is revealed by the many rock engravings and paintings which show species dependent upon water (such as hippopotamus), as well as species which have been extinct from the region for at least several thousand years (buffalo, elephant, rhino, giraffe); more recent paintings show cattle herders, which may have helped bring about the drier conditions in this part of the Sahara. The ancient art works are of outstanding interest in demonstrating a long-extinct relationship between man and his environment.

   Criteria: (ii), (iii), plus cultural criteria

2. **Name of property**: OKAVANGO DELTA

   Country: Botswana

   Universal significance: This inland delta supports one of the richest faunas in southern Africa, forming a permanent source of water in the midst of arid habitats; it is comparable only to Sudan's Sudd as an important wetland. It has its source in the Angola highlands, with internal drainage. It supports, among many others, hippo, sitatunga, sable, roan, elephant, and crocodile, as well as migratory birds and, in particular, waterfowl populations of outstanding interest, such as slaty egret, a species of very restricted distribution elsewhere. The site is now seriously threatened by endosulphan pesticide spraying aimed at eradicating the tse-tse fly (at a cost of $6 million).

   Criteria: (ii), (iii), (iv)

3. **Name of property**: CENTRAL KALAHARI GAME RESERVE

   Country: Botswana

   Universal significance: This game reserve comprises 5,280,000 hectares, and contains the best combination in Africa of animal species adapted to semi-arid conditions and hunting-and-gathering human groups (the Kalahari Bushmen). It is likely to be subdivided for livestock, but a large portion should be zoned for conservation.

   Criteria: (ii), (iii), plus cultural criteria

4. **Name of property**: MT. CAMEROON

   Country: Cameroon

   Universal significance: Mt. Cameroon (4070 m) is an outstanding representative of the Guinean Highlands, with a high degree of endemism of plants and animals; 22 species of birds are found only on Mt. Cameroon, and another 29 birds have isolated (and often clearly subspeciated) populations on the mountain. It was a Pleistocene forest refuge during dry periods and a source of colonizers during wetter periods. It would qualify for consideration for the "World Heritage in Danger" list, as it is not now protected and its forests are being eaten away by shifting cultivators and will soon lose its value.

   Criteria: (ii), (iii), (iv)

5. **Name of property**: DJA FOREST RESERVE

   Country: Cameroon

   Universal significance: This site, covering 526,000 ha, is a large tract of lowland tropical rainforest, one of the world's most threatened biomes. It contains some 14 species of primates, including the endangered lowland gorilla and chimpanzee. It is also inhabited by Pygmy hunting societies. The site is a Biosphere Reserve.

   Criteria: (ii), (iii), (iv), plus cultural criteria

6. **Name of property**: MT. NIMBA STRICT NATURE RESERVE (Guinea portion elected WHS 1980)

   Country: Guinea, Ivory Coast and Liberia

   Universal significance: Comprising 18,000 hectares between the three countries, Mt. Nimba was a Pleistocene forest refuge, with a remarkably rich endemic flora and fauna. The lower slopes are covered in dense semi-deciduous forest, giving way, above 1000 m, to montane forest rich in epiphytes. The summits of this long, iron-rich mountain are covered in montane savanna. An amphibian of special interest is a toad which occurs in the montane savannas and gives birth to live young (rather than laying eggs like most toads).

   Criteria: (ii), (iii), (iv)

7. **Name of property**: THE AFAR TRIANGLE

   Country: Ethiopia and Djibouti

   Universal significance: The Afar Triangle is of extreme geological importance, the world's only terrestrial focal point for new oceans in the making. A wild and rugged country, with deserts below sea level,

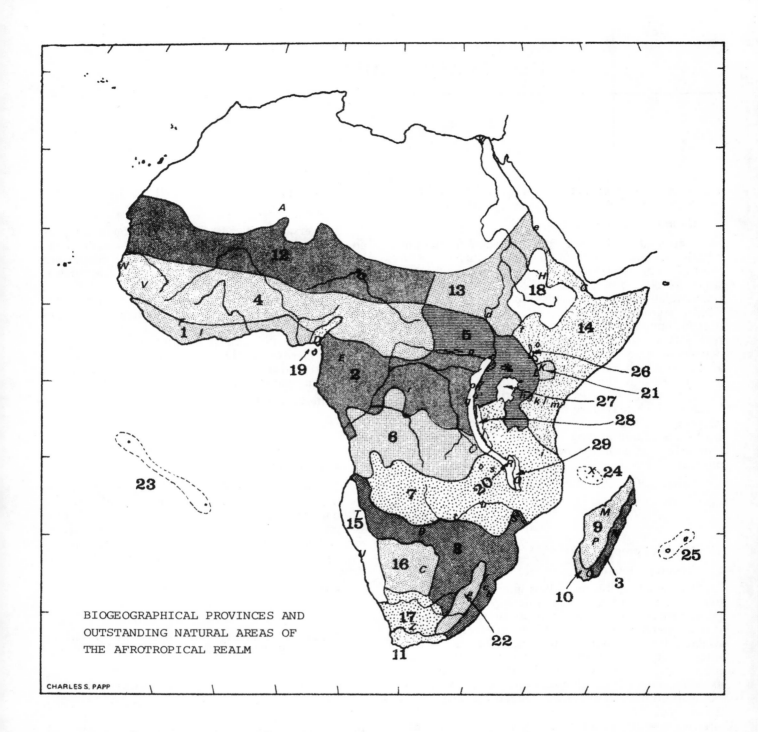

BIOGEOGRAPHICAL PROVINCES AND
OUTSTANDING NATURAL AREAS OF
THE AFROTROPICAL REALM

CHARLES S. PAPP

towering escarpments, fissures, volcanoes, and craters, the Afar region is the meeting point of the Gulf of Aden and Red Sea rifts, which are perpendicular to each other; and it is the northern terminal of the great rift system running down eastern Africa. Many of the basic discoveries of the processes of plate tectonics have been based on the geology of the Afar Triangle.

Criteria: (ii), (iii)

8. **Name of property**: SIMIEN MOUNTAINS NATIONAL PARK (elected WHS 1978)

Country: Ethiopia

Universal significance: This park of 22,500 hectares contains the most dramatic mountain scenery in Africa, with cliffs 1500 metres high inhabited by the endangered and endemic Walia Ibex. The alpine woods, heath forest and montane moorland is also the habitat of the endemic Simien fox, and the Gelada baboon is also endemic to this part of Ethiopia. Some 400 species of birds have been recorded.

Criteria: (iii), (iv)

9. **Name of property**: TAI NATIONAL PARK (nominated WHS 1981)

Country: Ivory Coast

Universal significance: The most important lowland rainforest site in all of West Africa, Tai is a 330,000 ha park which has been a centre of evolution throughout the Pleistocene, serving as a refugium during dry periods, then acting as a centre of dispersal during the moist periods. It has a high diversity of endemic plants, and supports a rich fauna as well. This site would qualify for consideration for the List of World Heritage in Danger. The site is a Biosphere Reserve.

Criteria: (ii), (iii), (iv)

MAP 3. OUTSTANDING NATURAL AREAS OF THE AFROTROPICAL REALM

BIOGEOGRAPHICAL PROVINCES
1. Guinean Rainforest Province
2. Congo Rainforest
3. Malagasy Rainforest
4. West African Woodland/Savanna
5. East African Woodland/Savanna
6. Congo Woodland/Savanna
7. Miombo Woodland/Savanna
8. South African Woodland/Savanna
9. Malagasy Woodland/Savanna
10. Malagasy Thorn Forest
11. Cap Sclerophyll Province
12. Western Sahel Province
13. Eastern Sahel Province
14. Somalian Province
15. Namib Province
16. Kalahari Province
17. Karroo Province
18. Ethiopian Highlands
19. Guinean Highlands
20. Central African Highlands
21. East African Highlands
22. South African Highlands
23. Ascension and St. Helena Is.
24. Comores Islands and Aldabra
25. Mascarere Islands
26. Lake Turkana
27. Lake Victoria
28. Lake Tanganyika
29. Lake Nyasa

OUTSTANDING NATURAL SITES
A. Tassili N'Ajjer National Park (Algeria)
B. Okavango Delta (Botswana)
C. Central Kalahari Game Reserve (Botswana)
D. Mt. Cameroon (Cameroon)
E. Dja Forest Reserve (Cameroon)
F. Mt. Nimba Strict Nature Reserve (Guinea, Ivory Coast and Liberia)
G. The Afar Triangle (Ethiopia and Djibouti)
H. Simien Mountains National Park (Ethiopia)
I. Tai National Park (Ivory Coast)
J. Sibiloi National Park (Kenya)
K. Mt. Kenya National Park (Kenya)
L. Aberdare National Park (Kenya)
M. Ankarafantsika Nature Reserve (Madagascar)
N. Perinet Forest Reserve (Madagascar)
O. Andohahela Strict Nature Reserve (Madagascar)
P. Toalambiby, Ampasambazimea, and Caves of Androhomana (Madagascar)
Q. Lake Malawi National Park (Malawi)
R. Nyika National Park (Malawi)
S. Gorongoza National Park (Mozambique)
T. Etosha National Park (Namibia)
U. Namib-Naukluft Park (Namibia)
V. Niokolo-Koba National Park (Senegal)
W. Djoudj National Park (Senegal)
X. Aldabra Strict Nature Reserve (Seychelles)
Y. Kruger National Park (South Africa)
Z. Karoo Desert (South Africa)
a. Giant's Castle Game Reserve (South Africa)
b. Lake St. Lucia System (South Africa)
c. Umfolozi-Hluhluwe Game Reserves (South Africa)
d. The Sudd (Sudan)
e. Sanganeb Marine National Park (Sudan)
f. Boma Game Reserve (Sudan)
g. Ngorongoro Conservation Area (Tanzania)
h. Serengeti National Park (Tanzania)
i. Selous Game Reserve (Tanzania)
j. Lake Tanganyika (Tanzania)
k. Mt. Meru-Arusha National Park (Tanzania)
l. Mt. Kilimanjaro (Tanzania)
m. East and West Usambara Forests (Tanzania)
n. Ruwenzori National Park (Uganda)
o. Virunga Natinal Park (Zaire)
p. Garamba National Park (Zaire)
q. Kahuzi-Biega National Park (Zaire)
r. Salonga National Park (Zaire)
s. Luangwa Valley National Parks (Zambia)
t. Victoria Falls and Zambezi Gorge (Zambia and Zimbabwe)
u. Mana Pools National Park (Zimbabwe)

---

10. **Name of property**: SIBILOI NATIONAL PARK

    Country: Kenya

    Universal significance: Sibiloi, embracing Central and South islands of Lake Turkana as well as Teleki Volcano, harbours the last faunal elements characteristic of the northern frontier of Kenya, including elephants, buffalo, northern topi, Grevy's zebra, and oryx; Lake Turkana, now alkaline and isolated, was once connected with the Nile and supports giant Nile perch and a large population of Nile crocodile. The central island is the main breeding ground for crocodiles in Lake Turkana (though it has been severely damaged by local fishermen) and the southern island is a superb wilderness area. The uninhabitable Teleki volcano has a species of lizard which can withstand ambient temperatures approaching 50°C. The surrounding Suguta Valley is an important nesting ground for flamingoes. In addition, Sibiloi protects important fossil beds where discoveries of early human ancestors have been made.

    Criteria: (i), (ii), (iii), (iv), plus cultural criteria

11. **Name of property**: MT. KENYA NATIONAL PARK

    Country: Kenya

    Universal significance: The second highest mountain in Africa, Mt. Kenya (5,194 m) is old enough to have developed a large number of endemic plants and several endemic animals. The equator runs across the northern slopes, yet the mountain has permanent snow and glaciers, with adjacent alpine flora; vegetation is complex, with giant lobelias and groundsels of particular interest in the alpine zone. The site is a Biosphere Reserve.

    Criteria: (ii), (iii)

12. **Name of property**: ABERDARE NATIONAL PARK

    Country: Kenya

    Universal significance: This park comprises 76,619 ha of montane forests and moors in the Aberdare Mountains, much of it over 3000 m. The area is very moist, with numerous streams cascading from a high moorland, and rolling ridges covered with tussock grass, heath, St. Johnswort, and others, down through bamboo and montane forest. Giant forest hog, bongo, and colobus monkeys live in the rainforest, with other typical African wildlife roaming throughout the park.

Criteria: (iii), (iv)

13. **Name of property**: ANKARAFANTSIKA NATURE RESERVE

Country: Madagascar

Universal significance: The foremost protected area of Madagascar, this reserve's 60,520 hectares protects no less than 7 of the island's 20 species of archaic prosimians as well as other wildlife species endemic to Madagascar; notable among these are the Madagascan boa and iguana, whose nearest relatives are to be found in South America rather than Africa.

Criteria: (i), (ii), (iii), (iv)

14. **Name of property**: PERINET FOREST RESERVE

Country: Madagascar

Universal significance: Perinet is the best remaining example of Eastern Malagasy Rainforest and contains no less than nine species of lemur inhabiting a wide range of habitats, from forest to bamboo to lakeside reedbeds; these include mouse lemur, fat-tailed dwarf lemur, lepilemurs, brown lemurs, avahi, black-and-white ruffed lemurs, hapalemur, diademed sifaka, and indri. Unfortunately, the area is virtually unprotected, the forests are being logged, and hunting is common; the area would qualify for the List of World Heritage in Danger.

Criteria: (iv)

15. **Name of property**: ANDOHAHELA STRICT NATURE RESERVE

Country: Madagascar

Universal significance: This reserve is of exceptional interest and importance in that it comprises two entirely separate and widely contrasting zones, situated respectively to the east and west of the eastern escarpment, only a few kilometres apart. Visiting the western sector of the reserve has been described as "like stepping back into the Triassic", with its strange *Didierea* cactus-like forest which is considered as the finest surviving example of this endemic family of plants. The forest also harbours four species of lemurs, two of which – the crowned sifaka and the lepilemur – are endangered. The humid eastern section marks the southernmost limit of the Eastern Malagasy Rainforest. Both forests are being damaged, and this site would qualify for the List of World Heritage in Danger.

Criteria: (i), (ii), (iii), (iv)

16. **Name of property**: TOALAMBIBY, AMPASAMBAZIMEA, AND CAVES OF ANDROHOMANA

Country: Madagascar

Universal significance: Three of the most important sites where subfossil lemurs, aardvarks, elephant birds, giant crocodiles, tortoises larger than those on

Mt. Nimba Strict Nature Reserve, Guinea (also in Ivory Coast and Liberia). (Photo : WWF)

Galapagos, and pygmy hippos have been found with remains of extant lemurs and the humans who arrived on the island some 1500 years ago; this provides clear evidence that the extinct forms, many of them giants, formed part of the human history of the island.

Criteria: (i), (ii), plus cultural criteria

17. **Name of property**: LAKE MALAWI NATIONAL PARK

Country: Malawi

Universal significance: Lake Malawi contains by far the largest number of species of fish of any lake in the world; about 95 percent of the fish are endemic, including about 350 species of the family Cichlidae (roughly 30 percent of this family of economically important fish). The lake has a number of distinct habitats, including rocky shore, islands and reefs, river estuaries, sandy and marshy lakeshores, shallow shelving sand and mud-bottomed areas, and the deepwater open lake.

Criteria: (ii)

18. **Name of property**: NYIKA NATIONAL PARK

Country: Malawi

Universal significance: Nyika covers 304,385 hectares of the Nyika plateau, a long ovoid of gently rounded granite alternated with blocks of sediments. The plateau has a rather temperate climate in the midst of the tropics, allowing a somewhat more humid environment which supports a rich and diverse fauna throughout the year. Crawshay's zebra is an endemic subspecies; roan antelope sometimes form herds of 50; and several endangered species have healthy populations.

Criteria: (iii), (iv)

19. **Name of property**: GORONGOZA NATIONAL PARK

Country: Mozambique

Universal significance: Gorongoza's 377,000 ha comprises four different habitats: subtropical palm jungle; thorn scrub; wide, open grassland; and marshy land teeming with waterholes. Minor habitats include gallery forests along riverbanks, lakes and pools. The wildlife is typical for this part of Africa, with an outstanding attraction being the "Acampamento Vel-

Simien Mountains National Park, Ethiopia. (Photo: Georg Gerster, WWF)

ho", a group of abandoned houses now occupied by lions. Two species of crocodile occur, Nile and long-snouted, and about 340 species of birds have been recorded.

Criteria: (ii), (iii), (iv)

20. **Name of property**: ETOSHA NATIONAL PARK

Country: Namibia

Universal significance: This huge (2,227,000 ha) conservation area is situated around the 1,000 million year old Etosha Pan, now a flat, saline depression of 460,000 ha which floods during heavy rains. The salt pan desert then becomes a sanctuary for up to a million flamingoes of both African species, as well as thousands of white pelicans, all of which breed there. The arid savanna (420 mm annual precipitation) surrounding the Pan provides ideal habitat for rare animal species, such as the black-faced impala, the Hartmann's mountain zebra, the roan antelope and the black rhino. Springbok, Burchell's zebra, blue wildebeest, oryx and their attendant predators abound on the open plains, while in the mopani, savanna elephant, giraffe, eland, greater kudu, red hartebeest and the unique Damara dik-dik occur.

Criteria: (i), (ii), (iii), (iv)

21. **Name of property**: NAMIB-NAUKLUFT PARK

Country: Namibia

Universal significance: This is the largest conservation area in Namibia (2,340,150 ha) and encompasses the spectacular Naukluft mountains, the highest sand dunes in the world at Sossusvlei; the riverine forest of the Kuiseb river in the heart of a desert; the vast, open, gravel plains of the Namib desert, and the haunting beauty of Sandvis lagoon on the desert coast. The Namib Desert is as dry as the Sahara, but much cooler, with moisture-laden fogs drifting inland. Furthermore, the seasonal prevalence of certain wind regimes carries a nutritious supply of detritus into the "dune sea". At the juncture of wind blown detritus and coastal fog a finely balanced and intricate food chain of species has formed the most varied biota of any desert in the world. The high species endemism includes many forms which are specially adapted for survival under arid conditions.

Criteria: (iii), (iv)

22. **Name of property**: NIOKOLO-KOBA NATIONAL PARK (elected WHS 1981)

Country: Senegal

Universal significance: This 813,000 hectare national park is the largest in Senegal, containing healthy populations of endangered species such as elephants, Derby's eland, bubal hartebeest, leopard, and wild dog. Over 325 species of birds, 70 mammals, and 35 reptiles have been recorded. The area has been a site of human occupation for at least 100,000 years.

Criteria: (iii), (iv)

23. **Name of property**: DJOUDJ NATIONAL PARK (elected WHS 1981)

Country: Senegal

Universal significance: Djoudj is a 16,000 hectare wetland which is a very important site for migratory

Mongoose Lemur, one of Madagascar's unique lemurs. (Photo : J.-J. Petter, WWF)

waterfowl. Over 2 million species make seasonal use of the area, with pelicans a particular feature.

Criteria: (iii)

24. **Name of property**: ALDABRA STRICT NATURE RESERVE (nominated WHS 1981)

Country: Seychelles (Note: The main islands of the Seychelles are included in the Indo-Malayan Realm.)

Universal significance: Some 400 km from the nearest mainland, this 19,000 ha reserve encompasses the entire atoll and lagoon. Except for the personnel manning the research and meteorological stations, the atoll is uninhabited, but it supports a population of giant tortoises now estimated at 150,000, in addition to a number of other endemic species and subspecies of animals and plants. One of the most remarkable of these is the flightless Whitethroated Rail, which is probably now the only survivor of several flightless bird species, such as the dodo, which once inhabited the islands of the Indian Ocean. Green turtles come ashore in larger numbers than anywhere else in the Indian Ocean to lay their eggs, and the atoll protects the largest breeding population of frigate birds in the western Indian Ocean. The island has been called "the most scientifically interesting coral atoll in the world oceans".

Criteria: (i), (iii), (iv)

25. **Name of property**: KRUGER NATIONAL PARK (Transval)

Country: South Africa

Universal significance: Created a Game Reserve in 1898, Kruger covers 1,948,528 hectares and is the largest protected area in South Africa. With a rich mixture of habitats, the area supports a wide variety of large mammals, including elephants, white rhinos, black rhinos, sable antelopes, lions, and many others. Over 400 species of birds have been recorded. The integrity of the site is threatened by coal mining.

Criteria: (ii), (iii), (iv)

26. **Name of property**: KAROO DESERT (Cape Province)

Country: South Africa

Universal significance: The Karoo Desert is composed of ancient sedimentary rocks of continental origin, with the layers of sediment beginning with glacial tillites and ending with volcanic basalts, giving a geological history of the past 200 million years. Volcanic pipes are characteristic. Many fossils of dinosaurs have been discovered. The vegetation is Karoo Bush, a mixture of species derived from the tropics to the north and the subtropic Cape Bush to the south. No specific site is suggested, as a survey is needed.

Criteria: (i), (iii), (iv)

27. **Name of property**: GIANT'S CASTLE GAME RESERVE (Natal)

Country: South Africa

Universal significance: Including an area of 34,991 ha, this reserve conserves an important section of the Great Escarpment, with towering basalt cliffs and plateaux of cave sandstone in which occur rock shelters used by the bushman artists as sites for their rock paintings. Important fauna include the largest population of eland in southern Africa and a significant proportion of the nesting sites of the lammergeier. Vegetation communities are of great interest, ranging from *Podocarpus* forest and areas of [/Widdringtonia cedars to open grasslands and alpine communities.

Criteria: (i), (iii), (iv), plus cultural criteria

28. **Name of property**: LAKE ST. LUCIA SYSTEM (Cape Province)

Country: South Africa

Universal significance: This large shallow saltwater lake and its environs include St. Lucia Game Reserve, False Bay Park, Eastern Shores Nature Reserve and St. Lucia Park, totalling 118,543 ha, of which over 30,000 ha consists of open water. It is a unique area, with manifold scenic and scientifically important components. Vegetation is varied, from aquatic macrophytes, *Papyrus*, *Phragmites*, mangroves and swamp forest, to dune forest and sand forest. It has the largest concentrations of hippos, reedbuck and crocodiles in southern Africa and supports great numbers of birds including several rare or threatened species. Substantial financial resources have been expended on maintaining the essential link between lake and sea, through a long channel that had become blocked through silting.

Criteria: (i), (ii), (iii), (iv)

Etisha National Park, Namibia. (Photo : Dolder, WWF)

29. **Name of property**: UMFOLOZI-HLUHLUWE GAME RESERVES (Natal)

Country: South Africa

Universal significance: The whole complex, including State land between the two reserves, amounts to 96,453 ha and represents a conservation area of major importance, for historical, geological and biological reasons. With varied topography, rainfall and soils, the plant communities are extremely diverse with such interesting elements as *Ficus sycomorus* along rivers and other vegetation types of scientific value. Well known as the only area in which the southern white rhinoceros survived, and from which hundreds of individuals have been translocated in recent years, the complex also maintains the largest black rhino population in southern Africa. Valuable historical and archaeological sites exist within the reserve.

Criteria: (i), (ii), (iii), (iv), plus cultural criteria

30. **Name of property**: THE SUDD

Country: Sudan

Universal significance: The greatest of all African swamps, Sudd served as a barrier to the penetration of tropical Africa from the upper Nile. It regulates the flow of the Nile, with excess water transpired by the vigorous growth of swamp plants, including papyrus, source of writing paper for ancient Egyptians. Supports rich wildlife, including waterbuck, Nile Lechwe, and white-eared kob. It is an isolated wet habitat in the midst of savanna, but the effects of the Jongli Canal, currently under construction, are unpredictable.

Criteria: (ii), (iii)

31. **Name of property**: SANGANEB MARINE NATIONAL PARK

Country: Sudan

Universal significance: Sanganeb is the most important coral reef area in the Red Sea, located some 25 km northeast of Port Sudan. The atoll is characterized by steep slopes on all sides which exhibit terraces, spurs, and pillars in their upper parts; the outer rim encloses three lagoons of different sizes, depths and exposures, so Sanganeb has a large number of different marine environments. The area is not only of outstanding beauty, but is also protected from coastal pollution by its open-sea location.

Criteria: (ii), (iii)

32. **Name of property**: BOMA GAME RESERVE

Country: Sudan

Universal significance: The Boma Plateau, with the 135,000 hectare game reserve, is often considered the "last unspoiled big game area of Africa", comparable to Serengeti; however, the migratory species here are white-eared kob and the tiang (a local subspecies of the topi), quite different from Serengeti.

Criteria: (iii), (iv)

33. **Name of property**: NGORONGORO CONSERVATION AREA (elected WHS 1979)

Country: Tanzania

Universal significance: This is a combination cultural/natural site comprising some 810,000 hectares. The great Ngorongoro Crater, with its flocks of flamingoes and large population of resident wildlife, is unsurpassed for its beauty; the site also contains several other major craters, including the Empakaai Crater with its deep lake. Olduvai Gorge, where many of the most important discoveries of man's early ancestors have been made, is included in the site. Masai pastoralists also live in the area, carrying on traditional herding activities. The site is a Biosphere Reserve.

Criteria: (i), (ii), (iii), (iv), plus cultural criteria

34. **Name of property**: SERENGETI NATIONAL PARK (elected WHS 1981)

Country: Tanzania

Universal significance: Serengeti covers nearly 1.5 million hectares and supports the greatest concentration of plains animals left in the world, including 2 million wildebeest, 300,000 zebra, and 900,000 Thomson's gazelles. It also contains 2,700 elephants, 200 black rhino, and five major predators. The migration of the giant herds of wildebeest, zebra and gazelles is one of the most remarkable and inspiring wildlife spectacles in the world.

Criteria: (iii), (iv)

35. **Name of property**: SELOUS GAME RESERVE (nominated WHS 1981)

Country: Tanzania

Universal significance: Covering over 5 million ha, Selous has the largest population of wildlife typical of Miombo Woodland, a habitat type which has twice as many plant species as the savannas further north. It

The African Elephant, the world's largest land animal, protected by several World Heritage Sites. (Photo: Iain Douglas-Hamilton, WWF)

contains 100,000 elephants, the world's largest concentration, as well as 4,500 black rhinos, the world's largest concentration of this species. It is clearly the most important woodland-savanna reserve, providing an ideal complement to the grassy-savanna Serengeti ecosystem.

Criteria: (iii), (iv)

36. **Name of property**: LAKE TANGANYIKA

Country: Tanzania

Universal significance: This site includes the Gombe Stream Strict Nature Reserve, site of the famous research on chimpanzees, plus the new Mt. Mahale National Park, which projects over 20 kilometres into Lake Tanganyika from the top of Mt. Kungwe (2576 m). Lake Tanganyika has an extremely high level of fish endemism, including 142 endemics of 145 species of cichlid fish. It is the world's second deepest lake. This site would be most valuable if it could also include the sectors of the lake belonging to Zaire, Zambia, and Burundi.

Criteria: (ii), (iii), (iv)

37. **Name of property**: MT. MERU-ARUSHA NATIONAL PARK

Country: Tanzania

Universal significance: Covering 13,700 hectares, this park has outstanding scenery, including the pristine Ngurdoto Crater – a smaller version of Ngorongoro but without human occupation or even visitors; the crater has been described as "Africa in miniature". Mt. Meru (4,540 m) gives the park great floral diversity, the montane forests offering a marked contrast to the tropical rainforests surrounding Ngurdoto. The park also includes the Momela Lakes, remnants of one of the most spectacular floods in history formed when the Meru caldera collapsed.

Criteria: (ii), (iii)

38. **Name of property**: MT. KILIMANJARO

Country: Tanzania

Universal significance: Kilimanjaro is Africa's most scenic mountain as well as its tallest (5,963 m); in fact, it is the world's tallest mountain that is not part of a chain. Composed of three peaks – Kibo, Mawenzi, and Shira – that were once sites of eruptions, the mountain can be climbed without special equipment (though there are hazardous climbs to be had). The mountain is a natural focal point of East Africa and the source of water for much of the surrounding countryside. Many of the typical African species of wildlife are found on the mountain, including elephants, buffalo, numerous antelope and monkeys, and leopards (sometimes found above timberline).

Criteria: (ii), (iii)

39. **Name of property**: EAST AND WEST USAMBARA FORESTS

Country: Tanzania

Universal significance: Along with the Ulugurus, these form the last major areas of montane tropical rainforest left in eastern Tanzania, with remarkably high species diversity of plants and animals in a relatively small area. Endemism is quite high, up to

Mountain Gorillas in Virunga National Park, Zaire. (Photo: Jacques Verschuren)

100 percent in some invertebrate groups. As one of the two last patches of rainforest, the remaining Usambara forests are under considerable threat and would qualify for the List of World Heritage in Danger. A field study may be required to clarify which of the two Tanzanian rainforests is the more appropriate for World Heritage status.

Criteria: (ii), (iii), (iv)

40. **Name of property**: RUWENZORI NATIONAL PARK

Country: Uganda

Universal significance: This 220,000 ha reserve lies in the Rift Valley, and includes lakes George and Edward as well as the connecting 32 km Kazinga Channel. The park extends to the great cluster of extinct volcanic cones and craters on the lower slopes of the Ruwenzori range, the snow-capped peaks of which are sometimes visible to the north. Northeast of Lake Edward is an area with 78 explosion craters, part of a violent eruption some 7,000 years ago; the craters vary in depth from 15 to 150 metres and most are covered in forest. Wildlife includes tree-climbing lions and chimpanzees in the Maramagambo Forest, and large herds of buffalo, hippos, and elephant. Some 543 species of birds have been recorded, including 15 herons, 14 storks, and 50 birds of prey. The site is a Biosphere Reserve.

Criteria: (ii), (iii), (iv)

41. **Name of property**: VIRUNGA NATIONAL PARK (elected WHS 1979)

Country: Zaire

Universal significance: This national park of 809,000 hectares has an extraordinary combination of habitats, stretching from marshy deltas through broad savannas, lava plains and volcanic mountains up to the eternal snows of Mt. Rwenzori (5,119 m), the tallest of the park's eight volcanoes (2 of which are still active). The park has what is probably the greatest diversity of wildlife in Africa, with the mountain gorilla being most notable.

Criteria: (ii), (iii), (iv)

42. **Name of property**: GARAMBA NATIONAL PARK (elected WHS 1980)

Country: Zaire

Universal significance: This vast undulating plateau of nearly 500,000 hectares is adjacent to Sudan and harbours important populations of savanna wildlife. Particularly notable are the northern white rhinos, a seriously threatened species, and what are reported to be the world's largest herds of elephants (up to 600). Roan and sable antelope also occur.

Criteria: (iii), (iv)

43. **Name of property**: KAHUZI-BIEGA NATIONAL PARK (elected WHS 1980)

Country: Zaire

Universal significance: This 600,000 hectare park supports 200 mountain gorillas, an endangered species, in an area where they are quite approachable. Many other species also live here, including chimpanzees, forest elephants, and a wide range of antelopes. Of special interest are the pygmies which are still living a traditional existence.

Criteria: (iv), plus cultural criteria

44. **Name of property**: SALONGA NATIONAL PARK

Country: Zaire

Universal significance: This huge park (3,656,000 ha) comprises two halves, with the northern half primarily tropical rainforest and the southern half woodland savanna. Encompassing a large section of the central basin of the Zaire River, it is accessible only by air or water; annual floods keep the area actively changing. Its large size gives it a rich fauna, with many species which are considered endangered. Some small groups of hunting-and-gathering people still inhabit the area.

Criteria: (ii), (iv), plus cultural criteria

45. **Name of property**: LUANGWA VALLEY NATIONAL PARKS

Country: Zambia

Universal significance: Combining South and North Luangwa, this property covers 1,368,600 ha and contains what is often considered the heaviest balanced concentration of game in the whole of Africa. Strung out along the sinuous valley of the Luangwa river, the Park has broad grassy stretches broken up by mopani woodland, with high mountains on both sides. The many oxbow lakes support a rich fauna of waterfowl. It has a unique subspecies of giraffe (Thornicroft's giraffe) and is Zambia's best black rhino habitat; elephants are very common. The Valley Bisa people are subsistence hunters who still rely on the wildlife of Luangwa to play an important role in their culture. The area has been described as "an order of magnitude more important than the Selous".

Criteria: (ii), (iii), (iv)

46. **Name of property**: VICTORIA FALLS AND ZAMBEZI GORGE

Country: Zambia and Zimbabwe

Universal significance: The world's greatest sheet of falling water, Victoria Falls drops over 100 metres into a fissure in basalt nearly 1.5 km wide. Below the falls, the Zambezi river has cut a narrow gorge 150 km long through four horizontal lava flows which can plainly be seen on the sides of the gorge. A small patch of tropical rainforest has become established opposite the falls and is supported by its spray. The gorge is the breeding place of the small, sparsely distributed Teita Falcon. The site includes Zambia's Mosi-Oa-Tunya National Park (6,600 ha) and Zimbabwe's Victoria Falls National Park (58,300 ha), as well as the Donnstream Gorge now outside the parks.

Criteria: (iii), (iv)

47. **Name of property**: MANA POOLS NATIONAL PARK

Country: Zimbabwe

Universal significance: This 220,000 hectare park is Zimbabwe's best area for large mammals, because the Mana Pools, formed from the annual flooding of the Zambezi, provide a year-round lush habitat which contrasts with the surrounding dry country, concentrating game during the dry season and forming the destination of the annual game migration from as far as 100 km away. Endangered species such as black rhino, elephant, and leopard are abundant here, as are many species of birds. The scenery is outstanding, with the wide flood plain surrounded by massive escarpments. Consideration might be given to including in this site the Kariba Dam and Lake Kariba under criteria (ii).

Criteria: (iii), (iv)

Victoria Falls on the Zambesi River, Zimbabwe. (Photo: Dolder, WWF)

IV. THE INDOMALAYAN REALM

1. **Name of property**: THE SUNDERBANS

   Country: Bangladesh and India

   Universal significance: This vast mangrove forest along the shores of the Indian Ocean is fed by three great rivers – the Ganges, the Brahmaputra, and Meghna – and lashed by occasional cyclones from the Bay of Bengal. It includes a 260,000 ha tiger reserve in the Indian part while the more extensive Bangladesh section is mostly reserved forest but no actual nature reserves have been proclaimed. It is a remarkable habitat for tigers, and the rare saltwater crocodile is found there. Marine mammals include Plumbeous, Common, Irrawaddy, and Gangetic dolphins and the Black Finless Porpoise.

   Criteria: (iii), (iv)

2. **Name of property**: MANAS WILDLIFE SANCTUARY

   Country: Bhutan and India

   Universal significance: The Manas Wildlife Sanctuary in Bhutan covers 55,000 ha of Himalayan foothills covered with deciduous forest through which the Manas River debouches onto the plains of Assam. It adjoins India's Manas Wildlife Sanctuary and Tiger Reserve covering an area of 283,700 ha and they share a wide selection of fauna, including tiger, Great Indian one-horned rhinoceros, elephant, wild buffalo, clouded leopard, great pied hornbill and other hornbill species; many of these species are typical of the southeast Asian rainforest and find their westernmost habitats here. Manas Bhutan also has golden langur, an endemic species of monkey discovered only recently.

   Criteria: (iii), (iv)

3. **Name of property**: LITTLE RANN OF KUTCH WILD ASS SANCTUARY (Gujarat)

   Country: India

   Universal significance: This salt marsh on the west coast of India is the last home of the Indian wild ass *Equus hemionus khur*. Covering 490,000 ha, the sanctuary provides a habitat to some 800 of these interesting and genetically important relatives of domestic donkeys. The Rann is a flat, salt-impregnated wilderness where almost nothing grows; it is covered by some 60 cm of water during the rainy season, much of it blown up from the Kutch Gulf to the southwest by strong monsoon winds. These salt flats are interspersed with slightly higher grounds of salt-free sandy soils which support grass, shrubs, and a few stunted trees and provide the sustenance for the Wild Asses.

   Criteria: (iv)

4. **Name of property**: GIR FOREST LION SANCTUARY AND NATIONAL PARK (Gujarat)

   Country: India

   Universal significance: The 140 sq km national park is part of the larger lion sanctuary, which covers 1,412 sq km; it is the last home of the Asiatic lion *Panthera leo persica*, which numbered 205 at the last census in 1979. The sanctuary contains populations of a wide range of Indian fauna, including prey species for the lion such as nilgai, gazelle, sambar deer, spotted deer, and four-horned antelope and marsh crocodiles *Crocodylus palustris*.

   Criteria: (iv)

5. **Name of property**: KANHA TIGER RESERVE AND NATIONAL PARK (Madhya Pradesh)

   Country: India

   Universal significance: This site contains 45,000 ha of rolling hills in the Satpura Range, forming a vast amphitheatre some 8 km in diameter hemmed in by hills and covered with sal *(Shorea robusta)* forest interspersed with grasslands. One of India's most spectacular tiger sanctuaries, it also has the only remaining population of the southern race of the swamp deer, the barasingha; other species include sloth bear, sambar, barking deer, spotted deer, wild dog, gaur and blackbuck (the latter three being Endangered). Important research on the tiger and its various prey species has been carried out in Kanha.

   Criteria: (iii) (iv)

6. **Name of property**: KEOLADEO GHANA NATIONAL PARK (Rajasthan)

   Country: India

   Universal significance: This small reserve of 2,800 ha is one of the most spectacular concentrations of breeding and migratory birds in the world. Once the duck-hunting preserve of the Maharajas of Bharatpur, the site is frequented by migratory ducks and geese in winter and provides sanctuary for numerous indigenous breeding birds in summer, when the natural depression fills with water to become a shallow lake; openbill stork, painted stork, 3 species of egrets, white ibis, spoonbills, Sarus cranes, and many others have important roosting sites in Keoladeo Ghana and the critically endangered Siberian Crane depends on the area for its survival.

   Criteria: (iii) (iv)

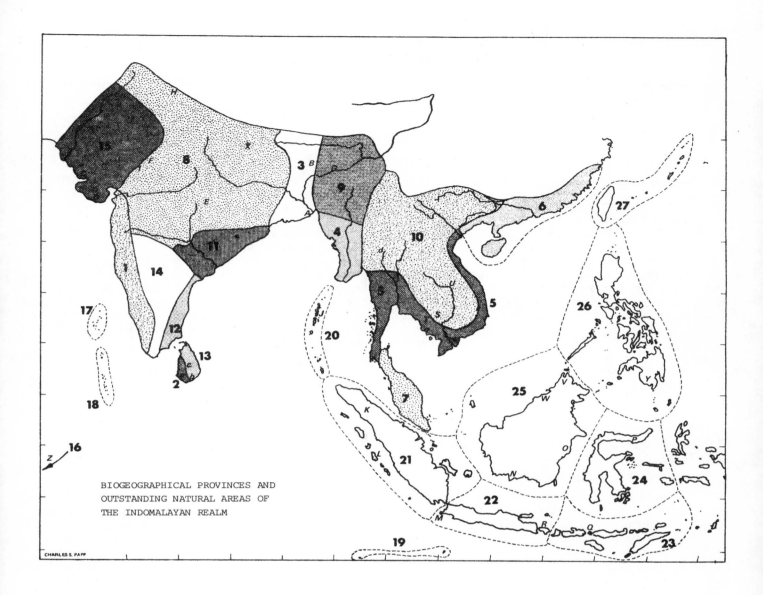

BIOGEOGRAPHICAL PROVINCES AND
OUTSTANDING NATURAL AREAS OF
THE INDOMALAYAN REALM

CHARLES S. PAPP

7. **Name of property**: KAZIRANGA NATIONAL PARK (Assam)

Country: India

Universal significance: This site of 43,000 ha is the best example of the Brahmaputra flood plain, where the mighty river is unleashed at its most violent each monsoon rainy season; the annual floods have prevented any human settlement, so the area is the best remaining habitat of the Great Indian One-horned Rhinoceros, supporting about a thousand of these archaic beasts. Kaziranga is a conservation success story, as protection has brought the rhino population back to a healthy state from a perilous low of just 12 individuals in 1908. It is also the best remaining habitat of the Endangered Wild Water Buffalo (an important genetic resource) and contains healthy populations of Elephants, Northern Swamp Deer, and Tigers (all Endangered).

Criteria: (iii) (iv)

8. **Name of property**: NANDA DEVI SANCTUARY (Uttar Pradesh)

Country: India

Universal significance: This is an outstandingly beautiful natural sanctuary in the Garwal Himalayas, with a virtually inaccessible basin surrounded by 6,000 m and 7,000 m peaks and capped by the 7,817 m peak of Nanda Devi. Containing a representative sample of Himalayan fauna, including snow Leopard, Musk Deer, Goral, Himalayan Tahr, and Blue Sheep, the Sanctuary was totally isolated from mankind until 1934, when explorers found a remarkable glacially-carved basin with rich pastures and a veritable Garden of Eden where herds of Himalayan ungulates grazed, innocent of all fear of man. While human penetration has destroyed the virgin nature of the site, there is still some of the world's most spectacular scenery and healthy populations of wildlife.

Criteria: (i), (iii), (iv)

9. **Name of property**: RANTHAMBHORE WILDLIFE SANCTUARY (Rajasthan)

Country: India

Universal significance: This site of 40,000 ha is a gem of lake and green vegetation surrounded by dry sub-desert country. The undulating Vindhya hills, with steep slopes and gently sloping flat lands on the hill tops, support lush deciduous forests with occasional open grasslands. Scattered pools and evergreen glades in small moist pockets remain even in the dry season, providing an excellent habitat for Sambar (which occurs here in its densest population, forming the only

MAP 4. OUTSTANDING NATURAL AREAS OF THE INDOMALAYAN REALM

BIOGEOGRAPHICAL PROVINCES

1. Malabar Rainforest
2. Ceylonese Rainforest
3. BengalianRainforest
4. Burman Rainforest
5. Indochinese Rainforest
6. South Chinese Rainforest
7. Malayan Rainforest
8. Indus-Ganges Monsoon Forest
9. Burma Monsoon Forest
10. Thailandian Monsoon Forest
11. Mahanadian
12. Coromandel
13. Ceylonese Monsoon Forest
14. Deccan Thorn Forest
15. Thar Desert
16. Seychelles and Amirantes Is.
17. Laccadives Islands
18. Maldives and Chagos Islands
19. Cocos-Keeling/Christmas Is.
20. Andaman and Nicobar Islands
21. Sumatra
22. Java
23. Lesser Sunda Islands
24. Celebes
25. Borneo
26. Philippines
27. Taiwan

OUTSTANDING NATURAL SITES

A. The Sunderbans (Bangladesh and India)
B. Manas Wildlife Sanctuary (Bhutan and India)
C. Little Rann of Kutch Wild Ass Sanctuary (India)
D. Gir Forest Lion Sanctuary and National Park (India)
E. Kanha Tiger Reserve and National Park (India)
F. Keoladeo Ghana National Park (India)
G. Kaziranga National Park (India)
H. Nanda Devi Sanctuary (India)
I. Ranthambhore Wildlife Sanctuary (India)
J. Andaman Islands (India)
K. Gunung Leuser National Park (Indonesia)
L. Siberut Island (Indonesia)
M. Ujung Kulon National Park (Indonesia)
N. Tanjung Puting Game Reserve (Indonesia)
O. Kutai Game Reserve (Indonesia)
P. Dumoga-Bone National Park (Indonesia)
Q. Komodo National Park (Indonesia)
R. Island of Bali (Indonesia)
S. Angkor Wat National Park (Kampuchea)
T. Elephant Mountains/Cardamon Mountains (Kampuchea)
U. Bolovens Plateau (Laos)
V. Kinabalu National Park (Malaysia)
W. Niah Cave (Malaysia)
X. Royal Chitwan National Park (Nepal)
Y. Rainforests of Southern Mindanao (Philippines)
Z. Valle de Mai (Seychelles)
a. Sinharaja Forest Reserve (Sri Lanka)
b. Yala/Ruhuna National Park (Sri Lanka)
c. Horton Plains (Sri Lanka)
d. Huay Kha Khaeng Wildlife Sanctuary (Thailand)
e. Langbian Plateau (Vietnam)

The Indian Tiger, a species found in several of India's outstanding reserves. (Photo : WWF)

The Great Indian Rhinoceros in Kaziranga National Park, India. (Photo: E.P. Gee, WWF)

known herds of this deer), Indian Gazelle, and Nilgai, along with abundant Tigers. The huge Rajput fort on top of the cliff which overlooks the main lake adds a cultural dimension to the sanctuary.

Criteria: (ii), (iii), (iv), plus cultural criteria

10. **Name of property**: ANDAMAN ISLANDS

Country: India

Universal significance: Located in the Bay of Bengal, the Andaman Islands have a fascinating wildlife and human culture; abundant undisturbed rainforest covers much of the islands, down to scenic beaches, fringing coral reefs, and abundant marine life in an area still unpolluted by soil erosion or industrial activity. Some 3000 species of plants occur, about 10 percent of which are endemic. The native people of the Andamans include pygmy hunter-gatherers of the type thought to have once been dominant in southern and southeastern Asia; particularly important groups which are in danger of cultural, if not physical, extinction include the Jarawas, Sentinelese, Onges, and Shompens.

Criteria: (ii),(iii), plus cultural criteria.

11. **Name of property**: GUNUNG LEUSER NATIONAL PARK (Sumatra)

Country: Indonesia

Universal significance: This site of 950,000 ha contains a wide range of vegetation and soil types, supporting Indonesia's richest fauna in any protected area; 105 species of mammals, 313 of birds, and 94 of reptiles and amphibians have been recorded from Gunung Leuser. Endangered species include the orangutan, siamang, tiger, golden cat, clouded leopard, elephant, Sumatran rhinoceros, and serow; for the Sumatran rhino and Sumatran orangutan, Gungung Leuser is the best habitat in the world. Scientific research has been carried out on a number of wildlife species for over 10 years. The site is a Biosphere Reserve.

Criteria: (ii), (iii) (iv)

12. **Name of property**: SIBERUT ISLAND (Sumatra)

Country: Indonesia

Universal significance: This island of 4,480 sq km has been isolated from the mainland of Sumatra for at least 500,000 years and its flora and fauna have evolved in isolation from the dynamic evolutionary events of the Sunda Shelf. About 15% of the plants are endemic to Siberut but the fauna has been even more affected by isolation, with 10 endemic species of mammals, including four primates: Kloss gibbon, Mentawai Macaque, snub-nosed langur, and Mentawai langur; each of the primates has retained primitive characteristics for their groups, making them particularly important for the study of primates. The bird fauna includes one endemic species, the Mentawai scops owl, plus 13 endemic subspecies; 27 families of Sumatran birds do not occur on Siberut, giving the avifauna composition quite a different character than on the mainland. The island also has some of the most interesting indigenous people found in Indonesia, with a prosperous hunting, gathering and gardening culture based on sago palm. This site is a Biosphere Reserve.

Criteria: (i), (ii), (iii), (iv) plus cultural criteria

13. **Name of property**: UJUNG KULON NATIONAL PARK (Java)

Country: Indonesia

Universal significance: This 60,000 ha national park is a triangular peninsula attached to the mainland by a narrow low-lying isthmus only 2 km wide; this isolation has protected what is the best fauna in all of Java. Foremost among the animals occurring is the Javan rhinoceros, of which 60 survive in Ujung Kulong (they are probably extinct everywhere else). Other endangered species include leopard, Javan gibbon, banteng, wild dog, Javan leaf monkey. The site also includes Krakatau volcano, the site of the largest volcanic eruption in recorded history; its eruption in 1883 caused tidal surges all along the coast of Java and Sumatra which killed some 36,000 people.

Criteria: (iv)

14. **Name of property**: TANJUNG PUTING GAME RESERVE (Kalimantan)

Country: Indonesia

Universal significance: This 300,000 ha reserve contains an outstanding example of swamp forests, varying from the mangrove forest at the sea edge through swamp and bog forest of several types. The reserve is noted for its dense populations of primates including orangutans, with a population density of 2 per square kilometre; at least seven other primates occur, including the spectacular proboscis monkey, endemic to the island of Borneo. Endangered species found in the reserve include clouded leopard, and false gavial. This site is a Biosphere Reserve.

Criteria: (iv)

15. **Name of property**: KUTAI GAME RESERVE (Kalimantan)

Country: Indonesia

Universal significance: This 200,000 ha reserve contains the finest example of lowland tropical rainforest in Kalimantan. There are many different forest types, depending on soils, water regime, and human disturbance. The flora is extremely rich in large trees: 180 species have been recorded in just 1.2 ha. The primate fauna is superb, with at least 10 species present including the Borneo endemic proboscis monkey and the Bornean gibbon, the latter with a population density of 12 per sq. km, one of the highest recorded; the orangutan population is also high, with a density of 3 per sq. km. Three hundred species of birds have been recorded, which includes 83% of all forest dwelling species reported from Borneo.

Criteria: (ii), (iii), (iv)

16. **Name of property**: DUMOGA-BONE NATIONAL PARK (Sulawesi)

Country: Indonesia

Universal significance: This 330,000 ha area is the best habitat for Sulawesi's remarkable assemblage of endemic species; over 90% of its terrestrial mammals are found nowhere else, along with 40% of its breeding bird species. Endangered species found in Dumoga include the babirusa, the lowland and highland anoa, the tarsier, black macaque, giant Sulawesi civet, and the Sulawesi phalanger. Another outstanding feature is the bird fauna, including two species of megapodes: the maleyo fowl, which buries its eggs in sandy soil near hot springs or other naturally heated sites; and the scrub chicken, whose eggs incubate in decomposing vegetation.

Criteria: (iv)

17. **Name of property**: KOMODO NATIONAL PARK (Nusatengara)

Country: Indonesia

Universal significance: This 60,000 ha national park is composed of three main islands (Komodo, Rinca, and Padar), located in the straits between Flores and Simboa. The reserve is famous for the Komodo dragon, locally called "ora". Discovered only in 1910, it is the most massive living lizard, with large males often weighing over 90 kg and exceeding 3 metres in length. With a total population of about 5,000, ora occur in all habitats, scavenging or hunting their own prey. The mammalian fauna is relatively poor, but it does include an endemic genus of rodent.

Criteria: (iv)

18. **Name of property**: ISLAND OF BALI

Country: Indonesia

Universal significance: This 400,000 ha island is one of the garden spots of the world. Its human population of 2.5 million has evolved a highly aesthetic relationship with the volcanic island; the rice fields and gardens are surrounded by protected mountains, sacred springs, and forests protected by custom. At the eastern most extension of the faunal realm of mainland Asia, Bali has the relics of typical fauna which until recent times included tigers. Bantang cattle, which are wild elsewhere in the world, have been domesticated by the Balinese for use in the fields.

Criteria: (ii), plus cultural criteria

19. **Name of property**: ANGKOR WAT NATIONAL PARK

Country: Kampuchea

Universal significance: While the main attraction of this national park is the incomparable complex of great temples from the Angkor Wat civilization, the wildlife of the 10,000 ha site is also significant, including Endangered species such as Banteng, Eld's deer, Tiger, Siamese Fresh-water Crocodile, and a wide range of others. It also shows the typical habitat in which one of the world's great civilizations evolved, along with the wildlife which co-existed with the mighty cities; some of the stone carvings show large concentrations of Elephants, abundant fish in the Great Lake, and the now nearly extinct Kouprey (the world's rarest bovine).

Criteria: (ii), plus cultural criteria

20. **Name of property**: ELEPHANT MOUNTAINS-/CARDAMON MOUNTAINS

Country: Kampuchea

Universal significance: Stretching along the southern portion of Kampuchea is a range of forest covered mountains with very high rainfall on the southern slopes which supports a tropical evergreen forest, and drier conditions on the north slope where there is tropical deciduous forest; on the Kirirom plateau is a natural pine forest, a very rare feature in this part of the world. Wildlife includes elephants, tigers, clouded leopards, and pileated gibbons, among many others.

Criteria: (ii), (iii), (iv)

21. **Name of property**: BOLOVENS PLATEAU

Country: Laos

Universal significance: The Bolovens Plateau has what is probably the most extensive and least disturbed tropical evergreen forest in the entire Anomite chain, with a rich endemic wildlife including douc languar, Lao marmoset rat, red vented barbet, bar-bellied pittar, and many others. Pilleated gibbons, elephants, tigers, and a number of other threatened species occur on this basalt plateau.

Criteria: (ii), (iii), (iv)

Tropical rainforest in Sumatra's Gunung Leuser National Park, Indonesia. (Photo: Fred Kurt, WWF)

Proboscis monkey in Kalimantan's Tanjung Puting Nature Reserve, Indonesia. (Photo : J.A. McNeely)

22. Name of property: KINABALU NATIONAL PARK

Country: Malaysia

Universal significance: This 71,000 ha site stretches from 150m elevation up to the top of Mount Kinabalu (4101 m). This is the highest mountain of Borneo, and contains a broad range of vegetation types, from the typical Malaysian tropical rainforest through mixed forest with conifers up to alpine vegetation related to Chinese and Himalayan species. With the rich vegetation, there is a similarly rich animal life, including some 12 endemic forms of mammals, several of them relics of the colder periods of the Pleistocene period. Over 400 species of birds have been recorded.

Criteria: (ii), (iii), (iv)

23. **Name of property**: NIAH CAVE

Country: Malaysia

Universal significance: This giant limestone cave 16 km inland from the sea on the north coast of Sarawak includes enormous populations of edible nest swiftlets and a rich fauna of bats. Humans have lived off the resources of the cave at least since the late Pleistocene, and the cave provides the best continuous record of human cultural evolution during the late Pleistocene-early Recent period; the earliest dated modern skull in Asia comes from Niah, dated 40,000 years old, and beginning about 20,000 years ago there is a continuous record of human burials of two types – flexed, seated burials without ceramics until about 4,000 B.C., and extended burials and cremations spanning the full Neolithic period from 1200 B.C. until modern times. The most important evidence of human stone tool manufacture and use in southeast Asia comes from this site.

Criteria: (ii), (iii), (iv), plus cultural criteria.

24. **Name of property**: ROYAL CHITWAN NATIONAL PARK

Country: Nepal

Universal significance: This 55,000 ha area of deciduous forest and grasslands in the Chitwan *dun* (interior valley parallel to the outer ranges of the Himalayan foothills) is drained by the Rapti River, whose annual floods provide a constantly changing mosaic of grasslands, riverine forests, palm thickets, swamps, and oxbow lakes. Probably Nepal's best wildlife area, it contains the only tiger population whose ecology has been closely studied over a long period of time. The park also supports about 300 Great Indian One-horned Rhino (its only habitat in Nepal and its westernmost distribution), Marsh Crocodile, and Gharial, the latter in one of the main surviving concentrations. Other important species include Gaur, Sloth Bear, and Leopard.

Criteria: (iii), (iv)

25. **Name of property**: RAINFORESTS OF SOUTHERN MINDANAO

Country: Philippines

Universal significance: The rugged mountains of southern Mindanao are covered in a dense and uncharted rainforest where a human culture known as the Tassady was able to survive undiscovered until the early 1960s. This small group of shy and graceful forest-dwellers has an intimate knowledge of the resources of the difficult forest habitat, being excellent hunters of small animals and birds and having an encyclopaedic knowledge of edible and medicinal plants. But these people are threatened by cultural disintegration as they are brought into the 20th century; their knowledge could be lost unless appropriate conservation measures are taken.

Criteria: (ii), plus cultural criteria

The world's largest seed, the coco-de-mer, found only in the Valle de Mai, Seychelles. (Photo: Christian Zuber, WWF)

26. **Name of property**: VALLE DE MAI (Praslin Island)

Country: Seychelles

Universal significance: The Valle de Mai is the habitat of some 4,000 coco de mer palms, one of the botanical wonders of the world. This palm produces the world's largest seed, whose large size and shape captured the imagination of early travellers throughout the Indian Ocean region. Just 18.5 ha in size, the site has luxuriant tropical vegetation which shows how much of the Seychelles must have been before human disturbance. The area also contains a number of endemic species of animals and plants, and provides a habitat for the rare Praslin black parrot.

Criteria: (iv)

27. **Name of property**: SINHARAJA FOREST RESERVE

Country: Sri Lanka

Universal significance: Sinharaja is the last surviving example of a viable size of Sri Lanka's tropical rainforest. As a remnant of Gondwanaland vegetation (descending from the time when the southern continents were all joined together), it has had an extremely long evolutionary history which is quite separate from that of nearby southern India. About 60 percent of the tree species are endemic (found nowhere else), and 16 of these species are considered very rare; many of the plants are of medicinal or agricultural importance.

Parallel to plant endemism, there are many endemic animals, including mammals such as the golden plam civet and the rusty-spotted cat (possibly the world's smallest), 18 of Sri Lanka's 21 endemic birds (including 3 which are endangered), and dozens of endemic reptiles and amphibians.

Criteria: (ii), (iv)

28. **Name of property**: YALA/RUHUNA NATIONAL PARK

Country: Sri Lanka

Universal significance: Nestling in the southeast corner of Sri Lanka, Yala is a curious mixture of rocky outcrops, scrub jungle, and plains laced with fresh water lakes and brackish lagoons; its eastern boundary is the sea, with high sand dunes and broad beaches. The backbone of the area is the Menik River. The 101,000 ha site is outstanding for easily viewable elephants and leopards, whose behaviour on an island lacking tigers is much bolder. Other outstanding attractions are the Sloth Bears and the plentiful and magnificent Peacocks. Sambar and Spotted Deer occur throughout the site, often in rather large populations. The area also supports two mammals endemic to Sri Lanka, the Golden Palm Civet and the Rusty-spotted Cat.

Criteria: (iii), (iv)

29. **Name of property**: HORTON PLAINS

Country: Sri Lanka

Universal significance: Lying in the uplands of central Sri Lanka, the Horton Plains is often considered the most scenic part of the country. Forest types vary from tropical rainforest to open grasslands, dotted with Spotted Deer, Sambar, and Elephants. About half of the plants are endemic to Sri Lanka, making this area very significant for genetic resource conservation.

Criteria: (ii), (iii)

30. **Name of property**: HUAY KHA KHAENG WILDLIFE SANCTUARY

Country: Thailand

Universal significance: Located in the remote hills of western Thailand, and draining into the famous river Kwae Kwae. There is a wide range of habitat, with dry evergreen forests along the river courses and mixed deciduous forest higher up, and dry dipterocarp on the ridges where soils are poor; there are also extensive open grasslands and scattered groves of bamboo of a number of species. The area is one of the wildlife treasure chests of the world, with no less than five species of macaque monkeys occurring within its

Asian elephants in Yala/Ruhuna National Park, Sri Lanka. (Photo: F. Vollmar, WWF)

boundaries. It contains the last herd of wild buffalo remaining in Thailand, as well as guar and bantang, three species of considerable importance as genetic resources. Tigers, leopards, clouded leopards and a host of smaller predators feed on the various species of deer which occur in the area, including the rare Fea's muntjac.

Criteria: (ii), (iii), (iv)

31. **Name of property**: LANGBIAN PLATEAU

Country: Vietnam

Universal significance: Located in the mountains of Tuyen Duc and Darlac provinces in southern drainage of the Sre Pok river, this is a very important centre of endemism for Indochina, including such endemic forms as the Langbian rat, collared laughing thrush, grey crowned crocias, short-tailed scimitar badler, and Germain's peacock pheasant.

Criteria: (ii), (iii), (iv)

V. THE OCEANIAN REALM

1. **Name of property**: MARINE LAKES OF PALAU

   Country: Republic of Belau

   Universal significance: Elevated above sea level more than 20 million years ago, ancient coral reefs have been eroded away to form the numerous salt water lakes of southern Palau. The salt water lakes form stable, small scale models of oceanic systems, each a naturally formed marine laboratory with different characteristics.

   Criteria: (i), (ii), (iii)

2. **Name of property**: VILLAGE OF NAN MADOL (Ponape)

   Country: Caroline Islands

   Universal significance: Built some 700 years ago, the village of Nan Madol on Ponape shows Pacific man as he lived in balance with his marine environment. The ruins spread over some 70 ha and consist of some 92 artifical platforms (some as high as 11 metres), each made of massive pentagonal or hexagonal pillars of basalt, built up from the shallow lagoon on the eastern side of the island and separated by canals for transportation. The most spectacular monument is the chiefly burial of Nan Douwas, sometimes considered the most remarkable example of prehistoric stone architecture known from anywhere in Oceania; covering an area 60 by 65 metres and protected by walls 10.5 m high and 8.5 m thick, the structure contains a number of separate tombs built of basalt prisms and containing a great wealth of archaeological materials which allow scientists to reconstruct the life of these ancient mariners.

   Criteria: (ii), plus cultural criteria.

3. **Name of property**: RAPA NUI NATIONAL PARK

   Country: Chile

   Universal significance: This 6,800 ha national park consists of the famous "Easter Island", with fascinating remains of an extinct megalithic culture which worked the volcanic rocks into giant statues which were erected throughout the island. There are also numerous smaller carvings, many depicting the sea birds on which the people depended for food. The scenery is spectacular, with volcanoes and rugged coastlines; being located far from any mainland, Rapa Nui has developed a number of endemic species, including about a third of its plants.

   Criteria: (ii), (iii), (iv), plus cultural criteria.

4. **Name of property**: ISLAND OF TAHITI

   Country: France (French Polynesia)

   Universal significance: Tahiti is the quintessence of romantic Polynesia. Seen from the sea, it is a wild, rugged, untamed island, with volcanic peaks towering into the sky. Surrounded by a protective reef and calm lagoon, the coastal lowlands have been settled by Polynesians for perhaps a thousand years. But the bulk of the island is a precipitous wilderness, covered in verdant vegetation which is virtually impenetrable; giant tree ferns, wild bananas, and magnificent chestnuts cover the mountainsides. Of particular scenic interest – once the colourful coastline has been left behind – is Lake Vaihiria, the only high volcanic lake in Polynesia. Some 500 m above sea level, the lake is said by local people to be bottomless; it is populated by giant black eels, thick as a man's thigh.

   Criteria: (ii), (iii)

5. **Name of property**: GUNUNG JAYA NATURE RESERVE (Irian Jaya)

   Country: Indonesia

   Universal significance: This 2 million ha reserve stretches from sandy tropical beaches to the permanently snow-clad summit of Mt. Jaya, at 5,030 m the highest point in Southeast Asia and the highest insular mountain in the world. It includes the widest range of vegetation classes possible in Indonesia, ranging from lowland rainforest up to ephemeral forbland. It has a large number of New Guinea's endemic species, including the monotreme echidna and a wide variety of marsupials, including forest wallaby, marsupial cat, tree kangaroo, and many others. Although no census of birds has been undertaken, the reserve is known to contain a number of birds of paradise, cassowaries, bower birds, crowned pigeons, and many species of parrots, cockatoos, and lories.

   Criteria: (i), (ii), (iii), (iv)

6. **Name of property**: FOJA MOUNTAINS

   Country: Indonesia (Irian Jaya)

   Universal significance: This area is a unique example of a tropical mountain range totally undisturbed by man, with tame mammals and an endemic species of bowerbird. Dominated by species of *Araucaria, Nothofagus, Podocarpus,* and various oaks the forest is draped with moss, lichens, and epiphytes. While there are sparse human populations in the adjacent lowlands, the Foja mountains are so rugged that there is no evidence that humans had ever visited the region until a small expedition in 1979 discovered, for the first time in the wild, the Yellow-fronted Gardener Bowerbird *(Amblyornis flavifrons)*; with no human hunting pressure, the fauna is remarkably tame and easy to observe.

   Criteria: (iii)

7. **Name of property**: MEERVLAKTE

   Country: Indonesia (Irian Jaya)

   Universal significance: This site is a large (25,000 sq km) mountain-ringed basin subject to annual flooding; it is a superb habitat for crocodiles, fish, and

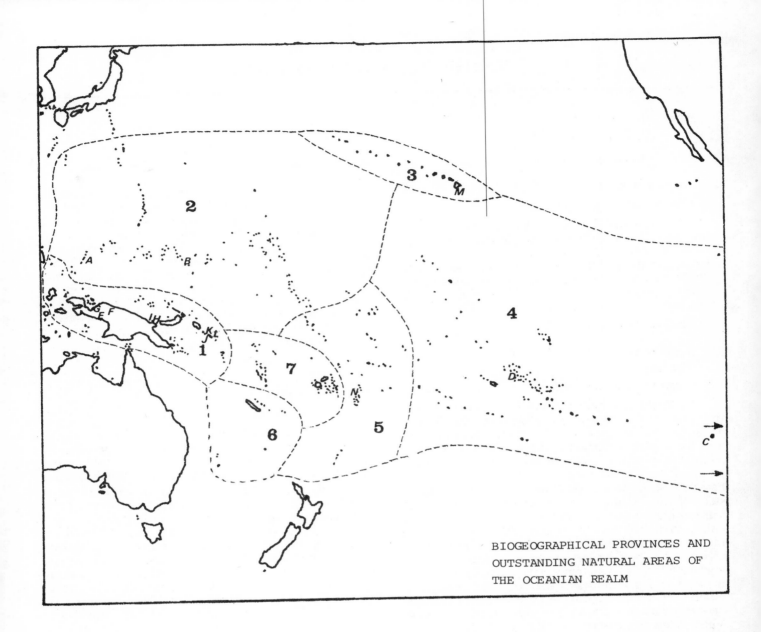

BIOGEOGRAPHICAL PROVINCES AND
OUTSTANDING NATURAL AREAS OF
THE OCEANIAN REALM

a wide range of waterfowl. The dryland forests support thriving populations of numerous species of birds of paradise, bower birds, giant pigeons, tree kangaroos, and many other species endemic to New Guinea. Due to its remoteness and difficulty of access, the area can be expected to be, within a few decades, the least disturbed area of tropical rainforest and swamp forest remaining in New Guinea.

Criteria: (ii), (iii), (iv)

8.   **Name of property**: LONG ISLAND

Country: Papua New Guinea

Universal significance: This site is a volcanic island that erupted and sterilized itself around 1700 A.D., leaving a large crater lake with a new hot volcanic cone in its centre. It is of outstanding geological and biological importance, being a relatively large island which is being recolonized by a pure tramp fauna and flora.

Criteria: (ii)

9.   **Name of property**: KARKAR CALDERA

Country: Papua New Guinea

Universal significance: This site is of outstanding scenic value: It is a striking vertical-wall caldera perfectly circular in form and 1,000 feet deep, set on the top of mountainous Karkar Island. This is probably the world's best example of such a formation.

Criteria: (iii)

10.   **Name of property**: RENNELL ISLAND

Country: Solomon Islands

Universal significance: This island is of outstanding geological, biological, and scenic value; it includes the world's largest raised coral atoll; one of the Pacific's largest lakes (the former lagoon, now home to sea snakes and possibly unique in that respect among lakes); home of numerous endemic bird taxa, and one of the westernmost islands colonized by Polynesians.

Criteria: (ii), (iii), plus cultural criteria

MAP 5. OUTSTANDING NATURAL AREAS OF THE OCEANIAN REALM

BIOGEOGRAPHICAL PROVINCES

1. Papuan
2. Micronesian
3. Hawaiian
4. Southeastern Polynesian
5. Central Polynesian
6. New Caledonian
7. East Melanesian

OUTSTANDING NATURAL SITES

A. Marine Lakes of Palau (Republic of Belau)
B. Village of Nan Madol (Caroline Islands)
C. Rapa Nui National Park (Chile)
D. Island of Tahiti (France)
E. Gunung Jaya Nature Reserve (Indonesia)
F. Foja Mountains (Indonesia)
G. Meervlakte (Indonesia)
H. Long Island (Papua New Guinea)
I. Karkar Caldera (Papua New Guinea)
J. Rennell Island (Solomon Islands)
K. Savo Island (Solomon Islands)
L. Kulambangara Island (Solomon Islands)
M. Hawaii Volcanoes National Park (USA)
N. Le Pupu-Pue National Park (Western Samoa)

Cloud forests are found in the upper elevations in Gunung Jaya, Indonesia. (Photo : Thomas Schutze-Westrum, WWF)

11. **Name of property**: SAVO ISLAND

Country: Solomon Islands

Universal significance: This island is composed of an active volcano with sand beaches, famous for the communal nesting grounds of the Incubator Bird *Megapodius freycinet*, which lays its eggs in beach sand or near the volcano where the eggs are incubated by volcanic heat or solar heating. The birds of this family (Megapodidae) are the only birds who do not incubate their eggs by body heat; most are chicken-sized, but their eggs are 4 to 6 times the size of a chicken egg and the hatchlings are able to fly immediately upon tunnelling out of the sand. These birds are under severe pressure from egg collectors throughout their range.

Criteria: (iii)

12. **Name of property**: KULAMBANGARA ISLAND

Country: Solomon Islands

Universal significance: This island is the classic example of a symmetrical circular stratovolcano island, over 1500 m high and home to two endemic bird species. As the timber industry is rapidly logging the lowlands which form the habitat of the endemic birds, the site would belong on the List of World Heritage in Danger.

Criteria: (ii), (iv)

13. **Name of property**: HAWAII VOLCANOES NATIONAL PARK (Hawaii)

Country: USA

Universal significance: This site includes a series of active volcanoes, which are under constant observation, research, and visitation. The site includes the Mona Loa volcano, over 10,000 m high when measured from its base on the ocean floor; this makes it the largest mountain mass in the world. A side volcano, called Kilauea, is constantly active, with sulphur fumeroles, steam vents and lava flows. The site

Hawaii Volcanoes National Park, USA. (Photo: 81st Fighter Wing, USAF)

also contains outstanding vegetation, including a tree fern forest, and protects a number of endangered species.

Criteria: (i), (ii), (iii), (iv)

14. **Name of property**: LE PUPU-PUE NATIONAL PARK

Country: Western Samoa

Universal significance: This site of some 2,500 ha is rough and wild, with poor soils. A lava tube 800 metres long, containing large populations of bats and swiftlets, is found in the centre of the site, surrounded by the best remaining tropical forest in Western Samoa; some 10 distinct plant communities have been identified within the park. Over 50 species of birds, reptiles and mammals are found in the area, including 21 found only in Samoa; 10 species are considered rare and endangered, of which 9 are found only in Samoa and find their most secure refuge in the national park.

Criteria: (iv)

VI. THE AUSTRALIAN REALM

1. **Name of property**: THE GREAT BARRIER REEF (Queensland) (elected WHS 1981)

   Country: Australia

   Universal significance: This 35 million ha site is composed of a long series of reefs separated by navigable channels. These reefs are composed of over 400 species of coral in 60 genera, with a wide variety of growth forms which reflect differences in exposure, hydrological regime, and other factors. The branching corals, massive brain corals, plate-like corals, encrusting corals and mushroom corals provide a diverse habitat for an unmatched assemblage of marine life, including over 1500 species of fish, 4000 species of mollusc, 242 species of birds, plus a host of sponges, anemones, marine worms, crustaceans, and many others.

   Criteria: (i), (ii), (iii), (iv)

2. **Name of property**: WILLANDRA LAKES REGION, NSW (elected WHS 1981)

   Country: Australia

   Universal significance: The most important site for investigating the period when man became dominant in Australia and the giant species of wildlife became extinct is the Willandra Lakes Region. Archaeological discoveries made here are of outstanding value, including a 26,000 year old cremation site (the oldest known in the world); a 30,000 year old ochre burial site comparable in age to similar burial sites in France; the remains of giant marsupials in an excellent state of preservation; evidence from 30,000 years ago that the people were depending on freshwater resources, among the earliest indications for this sort of human economy; and grindstones from 18,000 years ago which were used to crush wild grass seeds to flour, and whose age is comparable to that claimed for the earliest seed grinding economies in the Middle East. The Willandra Lakes system is thought by anthropologists to be as important to the global documentation of the culture of early *Homo sapiens* as the Olduvai Gorge is to hominid origins. The site also is a remarkable example of an extinct lake system, with a long series of lakes which became progressively drier in succession.

   Criteria: (i), (ii), (iii), plus cultural criteria

3. **Name of property**: KAKADU NATIONAL PARK (Northern Territory) (elected WHS 1981)

   Country: Australia

   Universal significance: Comprising 600,000 ha of tidal flats, flood plains and majestic sandstone plateaux and escarpments in the Alligator river drainage, Kakadu is home to a third of Australia's bird species and a quarter of the continent's fish species; of special interest is a primitive archer fish which is elsewhere known only from New Guinea, an indication of the ancient links between Australia and its northern neighbour. Endangered species such as estuarine crocodile, chestnut-quilled pigeon, and hooded parrot find secure habitats in Kakadu's rivers and forests, and a recently discovered python appears to be restricted to the stony escarpment country, as does a large gecko lizard. Kakadu is also a fascinating Aboriginal homeland, with over 1000 archaeological and aboriginal art sites having been identified; among these is the site revealing evidence of the earliest human settlement in Australia and the world's oldest edge-ground axe.

   Criteria: (i), (ii), (iii), (iv), plus cultural criteria

4. **Name of property**: LORD HOWE ISLAND, NSW (nominated to WHS 1981)

   Country: Australia

   Universal significance: The remains of ancient volcanoes that erupted on the western edge of an extensive undersea ridge during the Miocene period some 8 to 30 million years ago, the Lord Howe Island Group provides a setting of unmatched natural beauty, with wooded hills, golden beaches, the southern-most coral reefs, and a warm shallow lagoon which changes colour like an opal. Of 177 plant species found on the island, some 57 are endemic, found only on Lord Howe Island; among these are four endemic genera, including the only tree-sized member of the pumpkin family in the world. Uninhabited by humans until the coming of Europeans in the 18th Century, the island was a paradise for endemic species of birds; but lack of fear of human predators made these species very vulnerable, and nine of the original 15 resident species are today extinct, including four of the endemic species. Today the island is the habitat of one of the world's most endangered species of birds, the Lord Howe Island woodhen, a large flightless ground dwelling bird that resembles a chicken. Once very plentiful, there remain only about 30 individuals.

   Criteria: (i), (ii), (iii), (iv)

5. **Name of property**: SOUTHWEST TASMANIA (nominated WHS 1981)

   Country: Australia

   Universal significance: This area of about 770,000 ha comprises the Southwest National Park (a Biosphere Reserve), the Franklin-Lower Gordon Wild Rivers National Park, and the Cradle Mountain-Lake St. Clair National Park; together these areas comprise one of the last remaining temperate wilderness areas in the world. Among the outstanding features of this site are human remains of over 21,000 years ago, establishing southern Tasmania as the most southerly known penetration by man of the earth's land surface during the ice ages; a huge meteorite impact crater with silicate glass fields and 100 m of lacustrine sediments; a scenic wild coastline; and temperate rainforest, sedgelands, and alpine heath, which include a large number of endemic

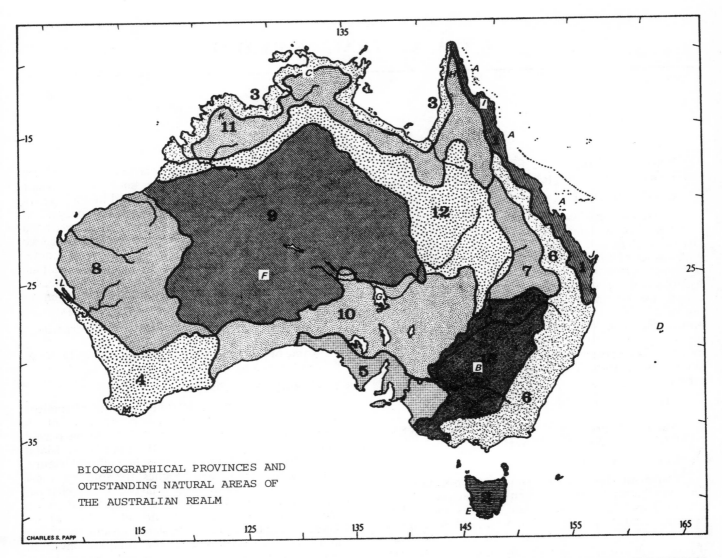

BIOGEOGRAPHICAL PROVINCES AND
OUTSTANDING NATURAL AREAS OF
THE AUSTRALIAN REALM

CHARLES S. PAPP

and endangered species of plants. The site also contains some two-thirds of the 32 mammal species known in Tasmania; many of these species are rare and endangered. If the Tasmanian wolf or thylacine still survives, then this will be the place where it might still be found. There is the possibility that this area might also be expanded to include the Walls of Jerusalem National Park.

Criteria: (i), (ii), (iii), (iv)

6. **Name of property**: ULURU NATIONAL PARK (Northern Territory)

Country: Australia

Universal significance: This national park (also a Biosphere Reserve), located southeast of Alice Springs, is noted for the famous Ayer's Rock, which has been called the biggest rock in the world. In fact, Ayer's Rock, like the adjacent Mount Olga, is a vestige of a sandstone mass which underlies the arid, eroded plains; it is composed of sedimentary rock which has been upthrust so that the grain is vertical to the flat plain. the brilliant colouring of Ayer's Rock changes from glowing reds in the light of low sun of morning and evening to the brighter colours seen during the warmer parts of the day. The Olgas were carved into their strange shapes by the action of water and wind, displaying rounded minerets, gigantic cupollas, and monstrous domes.

Criteria: (i), (ii), plus cultural criteria

7. **Name of property**: THE CHANNEL COUNTRY (Queensland and Northern Territory)

Country: Australia

Universal significance: This site of about 1.3 million square kilometres is composed of the braided sections of the inland ancient river systems that drain the catchment system of Lake Eyre (the world's 16th largest lake). This arid country includes the world's largest peneplained land surface; hot and dry, evaporation is intense and the sparse rainfall is soaked up as it falls – only twice in this century has rainfall been sufficient to fill the lake to capacity. The frequently-changing rivers and streams and wind-blown distribution of soil provide an outstanding opportunity to study the changing patterns of landscapes and distribution of soils.

Criteria: (i), (ii)

8. **Name of property**: CAPE YORK PENINSULA (Queensland)

Country: Australia

Universal significance: The rainforest of the northern Cape York Peninsula contains many forms of animal and plant life which are closely related with those of New Guinea; the dry and inhospitable Laura Basin prevents these tropical rainforest species from extending further south, so many of them are found in Australia only in these northern rainforests. Significant

MAP 6. OUTSTANDING NATURAL AREAS OF THE AUSTRALIAN REALM

BIOGEOGRAPHICAL PROVINCES
1. Queensland Coastal
2. Tasmanian
3. Northern Coastal
4. Western Sclerophyll
5. Southern Sclerophyll
6. Eastern Sclerophyll
7. Brigalow
8. Western Mulga
9. Central Desert
10. Southern Mulga/Saltbush
11. Northern Savanna
12. Northern Grasslands
13. Eastern Grasslands & Savannas

OUTSTANDING NATURAL SITES
A. The Great Barrier Reef
B. Willandra Lakes Region
C. Kakadu National Park
D. Lord Howe Island
E. Southwest Tasmania
F. Uluru National Park
G. The Channel Country
H. Cape York Peninsula
I. Queensland Rainforests
J. The Great Sandy Region
K. The Kimberlies
L. Shark Bay
M. Forest and Wildflower Regions

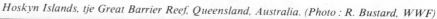

species involve the spotted and grey cuscus, the spiny-haired bandicoot, palm cockatoo, and eclectus parrot; the latter two are the only Australian representatives of their genera. Of Australia's three species of birds of paradise, two species, the magnificent rifle-bird and the mamacode, do not occur further south. These are the most colourful forests in Australia, with many species of orchids, flowering trees and vines, insects and reptiles; approximately 7% of the total Australian butterfly fauna occurs only in these forests. Also significant are the perched lake system at Cape Grenville and the sandstone country around Quikan which contains some of the most outstanding Aboriginal art in the country.

Criteria: (i), (ii), (iii), (iv)

9. **Name of property**: QUEENSLAND RAINFORESTS (Queensland)

Country: Australia **Universal significance**: The wet tropics of Queensland include the most diverse habitats in Australia, as well as some of the most superb scenery. These areas are characterized by deep gorges with fast-running creeks, black rock cliff faces, and silvery plumes of water falling from high rocky ledges. As a refuge habitat from when Australia was more moist and better forested, these tropical forests contain a number of primitive relict species; outstanding among these is the recently discovered *Idiospermum australiense*, a species which is the only member of its family and one which provides clues to the very origins of

Hoskyn Islands, tje Great Barrier Reef, Queensland, Australia. (Photo: R. Bustard, WWF)

Lake St. Clair and Mount Olympus, Tasmania. (Photo : WWF)

plants. The region also includes a number of volcanic characteristics, including craters, cinder cones, explosion pipes, and deep crater lakes surrounded by tropical forest.

Criteria: (i), (ii), (iii), (iv)

10. **Name of property**: THE GREAT SANDY REGION (Queensland)

Country: Australia

Universal significance: Australia, the oldest continent, has been exposed to enormous weathering to produce a great volume of sand. The most outstanding example of this phenomenon is found in Queensland, where the sand has been washed down fast-flowing rivers to the coast where it has been concentrated by wind and tide and heaped into massive sand dunes. The giant masses of sand are dynamic geomorphic processes which have been sculpted and recontoured by the prevalent south-east trade winds to form a rugged wild terrain which has been colonized and stabilized by tenacious, aggressive plant communities culminating in the development of rainforests, coastal heaths, and freshwater swamps; the most spectacular sight in the rainforest is to see massive trees growing on pure sand (nearly all of the nutrients – mostly derived from the atmosphere – are contained in the trees, not in the soil). Fraser Island National Park, which may be the most

important part of the region, is considered to be as important an example of sand masses as the Great Barrier Reef is for coral reefs. Fraser Island, also known as Great Sandy Island, is the largest sand island in the world, as well as probably the largest single sand mass; with Cooloola, it forms the Great Sandy Region. The coastal mangroves and seagrass meadows of this area also form important habitats for species such as dugongs and numerous economically important fish.

Criteria: (i), (ii), (iii)

11. **Name of property**: THE KIMBERLIES (Western Australia)

Country: Australia

Universal significance: This area, of some quarter of a million square kilometres, contains continuous mountain ranges, escarpments and plateaux, eroded by wind and flooding rain to form steep water courses, dry for most of the year. In areas of red sandhills, there is a profusion of colourful desert shrubs. Some 350 million years ago, the Kimberly region was an island surrounded by warm seas. In the shallow water surrounding the ancient island a barrier reef formed of stromatolites, a type of algae which still survives in a few places in Australia today. Over the years the areas around the reef were filled in by sediments, but erosion later stripped off the overburden, removing the softer

The Koala is an animal sympol of Australia. (Photo : WWF)

sediments more quickly and leaving the stromatolite limestone reef exposed, just as the original reef rose out of the bed of the sea over 300 million years ago. Another outstanding feature is the Wolf Creek meteorite crater, a deep, perfectly circular hole one kilometre across, with steep walls and a flat floor of gypsum (it has been established as a National Monument). In many places in the Kimberlies, there are aboriginal paintings of a style quite different from those in other parts of Australia.

Criteria: (i), (ii), (iii) plus cultural criteria

12. **Name of property**: SHARK BAY (Western Australia)

Country: Australia

Universal significance: Covering an area of over 500,000 ha, Shark Bay has numerous bays, inlets, and islands scattered throughout the shallow seas of the area. Interspersed sand banks and seagrass meadows support a profusion of aquatic life, including undisturbed populations of dugongs, green turtles, rays, sharks, and shell fish. In the highly saline waters of the Hamelin pool, high rates of evaporation and low rates of circulation have caused the formation of algal stromatolites, structures of blue green algal mats bound together by sediment; these formations are exactly like those known from 300 million years ago. Of particular interest are two islands contained within the site, Bernier and Dorre, which form the northwestern boundary of Shark Bay. On these islands are found several species of mammals which have become extinct on the mainland, including the banded hare wallaby, the barred bandicoot, the western hare wallaby (also found in one part of the Northern Territory) and the boodie, a rat kangaroo.

Criteria: (i), (ii), (iii), (iv)

13. **Name of property**: FOREST AND WILD-FLOWER REGIONS (Western Australia)

Country: Australia

Universal significance: This area, including a number of national parks, features a sandy coastline with limestone cliffs and sand dunes which have been carved into fascinating shapes by the wind. With a multitude of wildflower species, most endemic to this part of Western Australia, the area is a botanical treasurehouse; some 2000 species of plants occur here. Also significant is the Karri forest, composed of *Eucalyptus diversicolor*; the virgin forest consists of pure stands of some of the world's largest living things, towering up to 80 m in height. The Fitzgerald River National Park (a Biosphere Reserve) is included within the site, as is the Dryandra forest which provides the stronghold of the Numbat, the animal symbol of Western Australia and claimed to be the most beautiful of all marsupials.

Criteria: (i), (ii), (iii), (iv)

Tropical rainforest in Crater National Park, Queensland, Australia　　*(Photo : S.G. Wardle, National Parks Association of Queensland)*

VII. THE ANTARCTIC REALM

1. **Name of property**: MACQUARIE ISLAND (Tasmania)

   Country: Australia

   Universal significance: The crest of a large underwater mountain lying some 2,000 km south of Melbourne, MacQuarrie Island is noted for its outstanding natural wealth, wild beauty and hostile climate. With important populations of elephant seals (110,000 individuals), fur seals, gentoo penguins, king penguins, rockhopper penguins, and many others, the island is a paradise for sub-Antarctic wildlife. MacQuarrie Island also has an endemic species of penguin, the royal, with an estimated population of some 2 million birds; the largest colony of royal penguins contains half a million birds and is the largest penguin colony in the world. The site contains a Biosphere Reserve.

   Criteria: (iii)

2. **Name of property**: AUSTRALIAN ANTARCTIC TERRITORY

   Country: Australia

   Universal significance: In the lack of a detailed survey of what Antarctic sites are most appropriate for World Heritage status, and recognizing the problems of sovereignty implicit in Antarctic, this site is proposed as a symbol of concern that Antarctica has been represented on the World Heritage List. Included in the site are the Prince Charles Mountains and the Mawson Escarpment, with the largest valley glacier in the world (the 400 km-long Lambert Glacier).

   Criteria: (i), (ii)

3. **Name of property**: HEARD AND MCDONALD ISLANDS

   Country: Australia

   Universal significance: These uninhabited islands is the southern Indian Ocean are only 38 km apart, but are extraordinarily different. Heard Island is a circular dome-shaped volcano 24 km in diameter which rises to nearly 2,800 m; it wears an ice coat, 150 m thick in places, which flows down the dormant volcano to terminate in ice cliffs at the shore. Although lashed by some of the worst weather in the world, the McDonald Islands have no ice, with their rocky surfaces swept clean by howling winds which sometimes reach 200 km/hr; rain, snow or sleet falls on about 300 days per year. But these islands are called home by a number of species of birds and marine mammals who live on the rich marine life in the Southern Ocean. King, Gentoo, Macaroni, Rockhopper, and Chinstrap penguins breed on the islands, and Heard Island is the only known

Penguins are animal symbols of the Antarctic continent. (Photo : Eugen Schuhmacher, WWF)

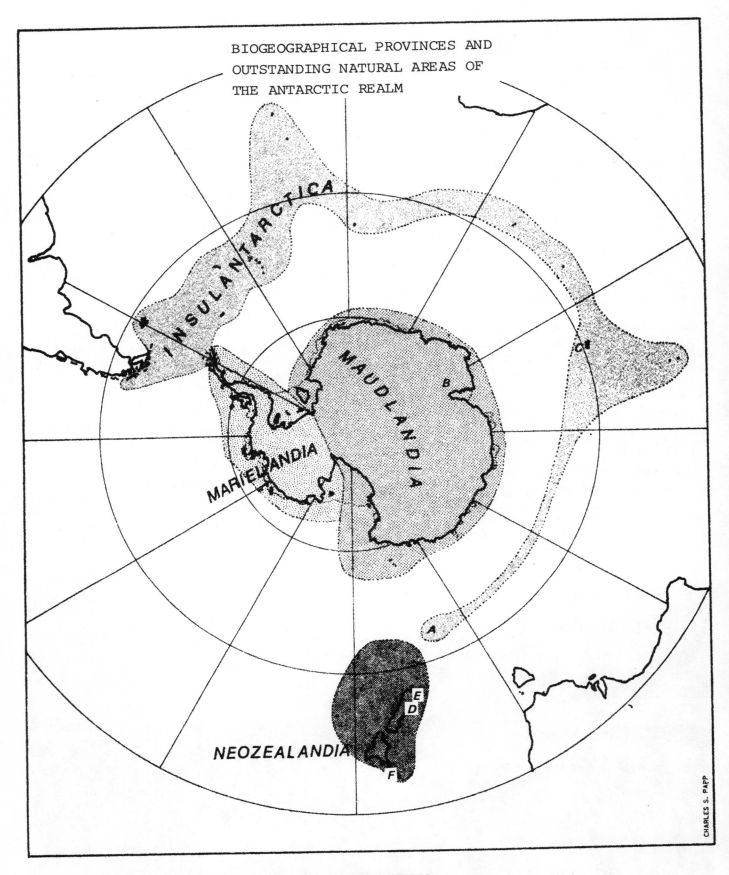

MAP 7. OUTSTANDING NATURAL AREAS OF THE ANTARCTIC REALM

BIOGEOGRAPHICAL PROVINCES

1. Neozealandia
2. Maudlandia
3. Marielandia
4. Insulantarctica

OUTSTANDING NATURAL SITES

A. Macquarie Island (Australia)
B. Australian Antarctic Territory (Australia)
C. Heard and McDonald Islands (Australia)
D. Westland-Mt. Cook Natinal Parks (New Zealand)
E. Fjordland National Park (New Zealand)
F. Poor Knights Islands (New Zealand)

breeding place of the Wandering Albatross. The islands are rare among sub-Antarctic islands in being free of the ecological havoc caused by introduced species.

Criteria: (ii), (iii)

4. **Name of property**: WESTLAND-MT. COOK NATIONAL PARKS (South Island)

Country: New Zealand

Universal significance: Mt. Cook and Westland national parks, together comprising some 150,000 ha, include the most spectacular glacial and montane scenery in New Zealand. The site includes Mt. Cook, at 3,764 m New Zealand's highest mountain; within the site are the Tasman glacier, one of the longest in the world outside polar regions, and two great glaciers which descend into temperate regions, a very rare feature in world geology. The mass of mountain barrier of the main divide dominates these rugged national parks, with Westland on the west and Mt. Cook on the east; the main divide of the Southern Alps acts as a barrier to the moist winds that sweep in from the Tasman sea, providing the exceptionally high precipitation which has created the glaciers and keeps them flowing today. The site also includes Lake Matheson, which provides crystal clear mirror-like reflections of Mt. Cook and Tasmin.

Criteria: (i), (ii)

5. **Name of property**: FJORDLAND NATIONAL PARK (South Island)

Country: New Zealand

Universal significance: This site of over 1.2 million ha provides some of the world's most spectacular wild scenery. Wild bush-filled valleys, scrub-covered ridges, sharp peaks, and breath-taking steep walled fjords that penetrate deep inland are features of this site; within the site is the Milford track, which has been called the "finest walk in the world", leading to Milford Sound where the dramatic Mitre Peak, an enormous triangular rock, rises sheer from the waters of the sound to 1695 m. Other spectacular scenery includes two of New Zealand's most beautiful glacial lakes, Manapouri, and Te Anau, the latter with a shoreline of 483 kms. Two of the world's rarest birds are found only within the site, including the takahe, a vegetarian flightless rail, and the kakapo, a large, flightless yellowish-green nocturnal parrot.

Criteria: (i), (ii), (iii), (iv)

6. **Name of property**: POOR KNIGHTS ISLANDS

Country: New Zealand

Universal significance: Poor Knights, 18 km off the east coast of the North Island, comprise two islands of 129 and 66 ha, plus numerous surrounding islets, stacks, and rocks. The islands are the heavily-eroded

Takahe Valley, Fjordland National Park, New Zealand. (Photo: WWF)

The Tuatara, a throwback to the age of dinosaurs, Poor Knights Islands, New Zealand. (Photo: P. Brennan, Auckland City Council, WWF)

remains of large lava domes, with numerous cliffs, caves and archways. The islands are now refuges for species rare or absent on the New Zealand mainland, including the giant weta, the endemic Poor Knights lily, and, most significant of all, the tuatara – a three-eyed reptilian throwback to the age of the dinosaurs which is the only member of its Order. The Buller's shearwater nests only on these islands, along with nine other petrel species.

Criteria: (iv)

VIII. THE NEOTROPICAL REALM

1. **Name of property**: LOS GLACIARES NATIONAL PARK (elected WHS 1981)

Country: Argentina

Universal significance: Los Glaciares is an area of 600,000 ha. which contains South America's most spectacular sub-Antarctic landscape of lakes, mountains, and glaciers. It is the habitat of the endangered huemul deer and the Andean condor, but its primary importance is as a site showing on-going geological processes, including glaciation; the Moreno Glacier occasionally plugs the channel between Lake Rico and Lake Argentina, causing flooding with cataclysmic "water avalanches" when the ice dam is melted. The site is one of the few areas in the world where glaciers are advancing instead of retreating. This area is similar in many ways to Torres del Paine National Park in Chile and could be usefully combined with that site to make an international site.

Criteria: (i), (ii), (iii).

2. **Name of property**: PETRIFIED FOREST (Santa Cruz)

Country: Argentina

Universal significance: This site of about 50,000 hectares contains a forest of petrified *Araucaria mirabilis* trees, with enormous fossil trunks which provide one of the world's best examples of a fossil forest. The forest also gives an indication of the climate in the area prior to the uplift of the Andes.

Criteria: (i), (iii)

3. **Name of property**: ISCHIGUALASTO-TALAMPAYA (San Juan and La Rioja)

Country: Argentina

Universal significance: Covering about 150,000 ha, this site is South America's most important fossil site, with the earliest known dinosaur fossils and some of the earliest mammals known. It also contains extraordinary geomorphological formations in an extremely arid part of the country; extremely well-preserved prehistoric pictographs are also found in the site, showing a long tradition of human presence.

Criteria: (i)

4. **Name of property**: CERRO COLORADO (Cordoba)

Country: Argentina

Universal significance: This small area of 5,000 ha includes interesting geomorphological formations with a relict forest in the central zone of Argentina which contains a number of endangered species. The site also includes important cultural values, including an extraordinary collection of pictographs and significant archaeological relics.

Criteria: (iii), (iv), plus cultural criteria.

5. **Name of property**: GREAT INAGUA NATIONAL PARK

Country: Bahamas (U.K.)

Universal significance: This 74,300 ha national park covers most of Great Inagua Island; a geologically very young coral island, it has never been in contact with the mainland and has developed a number of endemics, including 7 races of birds, 4 forms of lizards and snakes, and one freshwater turtle. The park harbours about 75 percent of the world population of the American flamingos, which feed and breed in a large (16 x 32 km) shallow salt lake.

Criteria: (ii), (iii), (iv)

6. **Name of property**: BLUE HOLE AND SURROUNDING ATOLLS

Country: Belize

Universal significance: The coral reefs of Belize rival those of Australia's Great Barrier Reef in species diversity, and the atolls of the Blue Hole region are unique in the western hemisphere. Fish life is very diverse, and the site provides important nesting grounds to several species of endangered sea turtles.

Criteria: (ii), (iii), (iv)

7. **Name of property**: HUANCHACA NATIONAL PARK

Country: Bolivia

Universal significance: This site of 541,200 ha is located in the east of Bolivia, covering a large mesa that belongs to the Brazilian Shield (Escudo del Brasil); it's an outcrop of Cambrian rocks which is of high geological value. Covered by a very humid sub-tropical forest, the area is very rich in fauna including such threatened species as Jaguar, Spectacled Bear, Ocelot, Giant Armadillo, Giant Anteater, Woolly Monkey, and Brown Howler Monkey.

Criteria: (i), (ii)

8. **Name of property**: LAKE TITICACA

Country: Bolivia

Universal significance: This area, comprising the world's highest navigable lake, is a unique high Andean ecosystem that supports a variety of waterfowl, some of which are endangered species. It is a special environment for humans and the cultural adaptations of the people are of universal interest. A joint site with Peru would be appropriate.

Criteria: (ii), (iii), (iv), plus cultural criteria

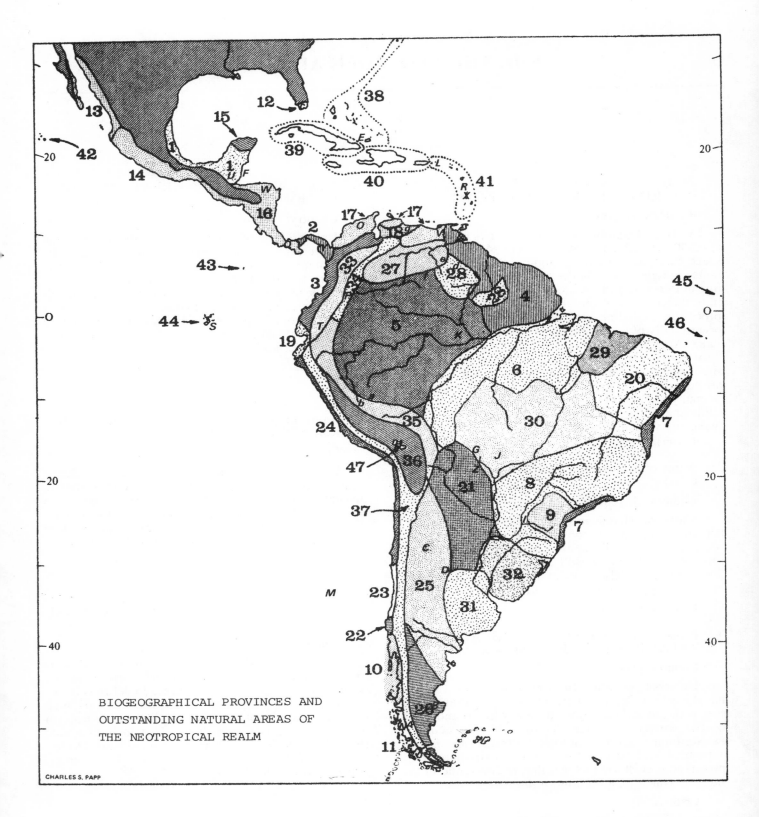

BIOGEOGRAPHICAL PROVINCES AND
OUTSTANDING NATURAL AREAS OF
THE NEOTROPICAL REALM

CHARLES S. PAPP

9.   **Name of property**: IGUACU NATIONAL PARK
AND IGUAZU NATIONAL PARK

Country: Brazil and Argentina

Universal significance: With a combined area of
225,086 hectares, the adjoining national parks in Brazil
and Argentina contain the spectacular Iguaçu Falls,
located where the Iguaçu river leaves the Campos
Cerrados of Mato Grasso. The falls are 4 kilometres
wide, divided into a multitude of cascades by rocky
islands covered in dense forests. In the words of Swiss
botanist Robert Chodat: "The waters of the deluge
falling abruptly into the heart of the world, by divine
command, in a landscape of memorable beauty, amidst
an exuberant, almost tropical vegetation, the fronds of
great ferns, the shafts of bamboos, the graceful trunks
of palm trees, and a thousand species of trees, their
crowns bending over the gulf adorned with mosses,
pink begonias, golden orchids, brilliant bromeliads and
lianas with trumpet flowers – all of this added to the
dizzying and deafening roar of waters that can be heard
even at a great distance, makes an indelible impression,
moving beyond words".

Criteria: (iii)

MAP 8. OUTSTANDING NATURAL AREAS OF THE NEOTROPICAL REALM

BIOGEOGRAPHICAL PROVINCES

1. Campechean Rainforest
2. Panamanian Rainforest
3. Colombian Coastal Rainforest
4. Guyanan Rainforest
5. Amazonian Rainforest
6. Madeiran Rainforest
7. Serra do mar Rainforest
8. Brazilian Rainforest
9. Brazilian Planalto Woodlands
10. Valdivian Forest
11. Chilean Nothofagus Forest
12. Everglades Woodland
13. Sinaloan Woodland
14. Guerreran Woodland
15. Yucatecan Woodland
16. Central American Woodlands
17. Venezuelan Dry Forest
18. Venezueland Deciduous Forest
19. Ecuadorian Dry Forest
20. Caatinga Dry Forest
21. Gran Chaco Savanna
22. Chilean Araucaria Forest
23. Chilean Sclerophyll
24. Pacific Desert
25. Monte Desert
26. Patagonian Desert
27. Llanos Savanna
28. Campos Limpos Savanna
29. Babacu Savanna
30. Campos Cerrados Savanna
31. Argentinian Pampas
32. Uruguayan Pampas
33. Northern Andean
34. Colombian Montane
35. Yungas Montane
36. Puna
37. Southern Andean
38. Bahamas-Bermudan
39. Cuban
40. Greater Antillean
41. Lesser Antillean
42. Revilla Gigedo Island
43. Cocos Island
44. Galpagos Islands
45. Fernando de Noronja Island
46. South Trinidade Island
47. Lake Titicaca

OUTSTANDING NATURAL SITES

A. Los Glaciares National Park (Argentina)
B. Petrified Forest (Argentina)
C. Ischigualasto-Talampaya (Argentina)
D. Cerro Colorado (Argentina)
E. Great Inagua National Park (Bahamas)
F. Blue Hole and Surrounding Atolls (Belize)
G. Huanchaca National Park (Bolivia)
H. Lake Titicaca (Bolivia)
I. Iguacu National Park and Iguazu National Park (Brazil and Argentina)
J. The Pantanal (Brazil)
K. Jau National Park (Brazil)
L. Anegada Island and Surrounding Waters (British Virgin Is.)
M. Juan Fernandez National Park (Chile)
N. Torres Del Paine National Park (Chile)
O. Sierra Nevada de Santa Marta National Park (Colombia)
P. Sierra de la Macarena National Park (Colombia)
Q. Amistad (Friendship) International Park (Costa Rica and Panama)
R. Morne Trois Pitons National Park (Dominica)
S. Galapagos National Park (Ecuador)
T. Sangay National Park (Ecuador)
U. Tikal National Park (Guatemala)
V. Roraima (Guyana)
W. Rio Platano Biosphere Reserve (Honduras)
X. Mount Pele (Martinique)
Y. Darien National Park (Panama)
Z. Defensores de Chaco National Park (Paraguay)
a. Manu National Park (Peru)
b. Macchu Picchu National Sanctuary (Peru)
c. Everglades National Park (USA)
d. Angel Falls and Auyan-Tepuy (Venezuela)
e. Cueva del Guacharo National Park (Venezuela)
f. Jaua-Sarisarinama National Park (Venezuela)
g. Henry Pittier National Park (Venezuela)

---

10. **Name of property**: THE PANTANAL

    Country: Brazil

    Universal significance: This area, covering 180,000 square kilometres, contains the largest concentration of wildlife in the Americas. The Pantanal is composed of vast alluvial plains between the Brazilian plateau to the east and the Bolivian plateau to the west, comprising the valley of the Rio Paraguay. The seasonal floods form many marshy areas in the Pantanal, providing superb habitat for waterfowl and grazing animals; the area lacks forest except along the borders, though the many isolated trees and patches of woodland serve as nesting sites for the incredibly rich bird life.

    Criteria: (ii), (iii)

11. **Name of property**: JAU NATIONAL PARK, (Amazonas)

    Country: Brazil

    Universal significance: This national park of 2,272,000 ha was created in 1980. The park protects an outstanding example of typical Amazonian tropical rainforest; the site is sufficiently large to support healthy populations of such species as the endangered jaguar and the giant otter, and the many rodents such as capibarra and ugutai; there are also at least seven species of primates, and birds such as macaws, curocaos and many others.

    Criteria: (ii), (ii), (iv)

12. **Name of property**: ANEGADA ISLAND AND SURROUNDING WATERS

    Country: British Virgin Islands (U.K.)

    Universal significance: Anegada Island, Horseshoe Reef and surrounding waters, totalling 13,000 ha, comprise superlative beaches and the largest reef complex in the Lesser Antilles, along with unaltered mangroves, cactus scrub, lagoons, and salt pond environments. There are a number of endemics, including an iguana, a worm snake, and the Anegada ground snake as well as nesting areas of magnificent frigate birds and brown pelicans. There are some 63 historic shipwrecks on the reef, dating from 1523-1825.

    Criteria: (ii), (iii), (iv), plus cultural criteria

The Pantanal is a floodplain paradise for wildlife in Brazil. (Photo: Hartmut Jungius, WWF)

13. **Name of property**: JUAN FERNANDEZ NATIONAL PARK

Country: Chile

Universal significance: 600 km off the western coast of Chile, is found the volcanic Juan Fernandez Archipelago (18,300 ha), the famous islands of Alexander Selkirk (Daniel Defoe's "Robinson Crusoe"). However, their contribution to biology is even more important than their contribution to literature, since they have an extremely high rate of endemism; over 70 percent of the Angiosperms are found nowhere else, and many of them have no clear relatives anywhere. A number of the plants are extremely rare, including a few known only from herbarium sheets. Because of the location, the islands form a meeting place for subtropical and Antarctic elements, a unique juxtaposition. The site suffers from the ravages of introduced species, and protection is incomplete; some 50 plants are listed as endangered. The site is a Biosphere Reserve.

Criteria: (ii), (iii), (iv)

14. **Name of property**: TORRES DEL PAINE NATIONAL PARK

Country: Chile

Universal significance: Covering 163,000 ha, this national park is located in the southern part of Chile, between the Andes and the Patagonian steppes. Its scenic qualities, including ridges, crags, glaciers, waterfalls, rivers, lakes and lagoons, are unmatched in Latin America. There are three great glaciers, all retreating rapidly (in marked contrast to Los Glaciares in Argentina). Vegetation is rich and varied, from desert associations to [/Nothofagus forest. Several threatened species occur, including the guanaco and the huemal. This area is similar in many ways to Argentina's Los Glaciares and could be usefully combined with that site to make an international site. The site is a Biosphere Reserve.

Criteria: (i), (ii), (iii), (iv), plus cultural criteria.

15. **Name of property**: SIERRA NEVADA DE SANTA MARTA NATIONAL PARK

Country: Colombia

Universal significance: This national park, covering 383,000 ha, is the most outstanding example of an intertropical montane environment, with perpetual snows; it includes Bolivar Peak, Colombia's highest, with superb Andean examples of glaciation. It also has important archaeological sites and biological importance. Settlements on the lower slopes are causing concern, and the fauna is rather scarce and shy.

Criteria: (ii), (iii)

16. **Name of property**: SIERRA DE LA MACARENA NATIONAL PARK

Country: Colombia

Universal significance: This national park in an isolated mountain range covers over 500,000 ha in the Andean cordillera and includes an unmatched series of biotic elements from Andean to Orinocan, Amazonian,

Wildlife of Galapagos National Park, Ecuador. (Photo: Heinz Sielmann, WWF)

and Guyanan; it probably contains the greatest diversity of wildlife of any area in the Neotropics. Threatened species include jaguar, spectacled bear, giant otter, harpy eagle, and Orinocan crocodile. Although the area is potentially outstanding, it is being severely damaged by human settlements and a new survey is urgently required. The site is a Biosphere Reserve.

Criteria: (ii), (iii)

17. **Name of property**: AMISTAD (FRIENDSHIP) INTERNATIONAL PARK

Country: Costa Rica and Panama

Universal significance: With 250,000 ha on the Costa Rican side and 200,000 ha on the Panamanian side, this site forms a vast area of tropical rainforest containing a number of endangered species of wildlife.

The Quetztal, the bird symbol of ancient Central American civilizations. (Photo: Clyde H. Smith, WWF)

Because of its size and diversity of elevation, rainfall, and soil types, it comprises a great number of habitat types, giving it unmatched species diversity in Central America.

Criteria: (ii), (iii) (iv)

18. **Name of property**: MORNE TROIS PITONS NATIONAL PARK

Country: Dominica

Universal significance: This site, covering 6,840 ha in the central and southern mountains of the island, comprises the largest area of unaltered cloud, rain, and moist forest in the Lesser Antilles. Centred on the remains of a young volcanic pile, it has superlative scenery, with four volcanoes, sulphur vents, mud pools, and the world's second largest boiling lake; this lake presents an awesome sight as the water at a rolling boil gives off great clouds of steam and acrid gases. It is the habitat of endangered Imperial (or Sisserou) and Red-necked parrots.

Criteria: (ii), (iii), (iv)

19. **Name of property**: GALAPAGOS NATIONAL PARK (elected WHS 1978)

Country: Ecuador

Universal significance: Galapagos National Park (691,200 ha) is world famous as the place where Charles Darwin made the natural history investigations that led to his theory of evolution through natural selection. The Park's wildlife is incredibly tame, so it is easy to approach such endemic species as giant tortoise, Galapagos hawk, and marine iguana. Some 77 of the park's 89 species of breeding birds are endemic, including 13 species of Darwin's finches, "whose radiation is such an eloquent expression of evolution".

Criteria: (i), (ii), (iii), (iv)

20. **Name of property**: SANGAY NATIONAL PARK

Country: Ecuador

Universal significance: Sangay covers 272,000 ha of diverse and complex ecosystems ranging from tropical rainforests to snow-peaked mountains; fauna is particularly rich, including threatened species such as woolly tapir, puma, jaguar, spectacled bear, Andean cock-of-the-rock, and condor. Sangay is considered to have been continuously active for the longest period of time of any volcano in the world.

Criteria: (i), (ii), (iii), (iv)

21. **Name of property**: TIKAL NATIONAL PARK (elected WHS 1979)

Country: Guatemala

Universal significance: Tikal National Park (57,600 ha) is both a natural and a cultural site; the famous Mayan ruins are the outstanding example of that pre-Columbian culture, with temples, pyramids, houses and sculptures. Large areas remain to be excavated. The forest is transitional from dry to wet conditions and supports a rich fauna, including 54 species of mammal; threatened species include jaguar, ocelot, Baird's tapir, and giant anteater. There are 303 species of birds, representing 63 of the 74 families found in the country.

Criteria: (ii), (iv), plus cultural criteria

22. **Name of property**: RORAIMA

Country: Guyana

Universal significance: This site, covering 220,000 ha located at the joint boundary of Guyana, Brazil, and Venezuela, is a temperate enclave in the middle of the tropics. Rising to 9,219 feet, Mt. Roraima is a red sandstone table mountain, with an uppermost plateau covering about 40 square kilometres with an incredibly complex relief; deep furrows, ravines, and sandy swamps provide a number of micro-habitats for plants and animals. The mountain is surrounded by cloud forest with low, gnarled trees of many species; seasonal forests and dry evergreen forests also occur.

Criteria: (ii), (iii), (iv)

23. **Name of property**: RIO PLATANO BIOSPHERE RESERVE (nominated WHS 1981)

Country: Honduras

Universal significance: This site, covering 350,000 ha, ranges from the coast of the Caribbean (with estuaries and mangroves) to a mountainous region topped by Punta Piedra (1326 m). The area has rich vegetation, including a number of plant relatives of domesticated varieties. The fauna of 39 species of larger mammals, 377 species of birds, and 126 species of reptiles and amphibians contains a number of threatened species, including the Caribbean manatee, Baird's tapir, and 3 species of cats. There are two groups of Indian (Paya and Miskito) of great ethnographic importance.

Criteria: (ii), (iv), plus cultural criteria.

24. **Name of property**: MOUNT PELE

Country: Martinique (France)

Universal significance: This site, comprising 5,000 ha on the northwest portion of the island, was the site of a volcanic eruption that produced a "nué ardienne" or gas cloud that wiped out the entire town of St. Pierre in the late 1800s; it is often cited as a classic example of such a gas cloud. The site has an unaltered and uninterrupted transect of flora and fauna after the recent volcanic episodes, from rocky coastal and marine environments to dry forests, followed by moist forest, rainforest, and cloud forest; it thus provides a classic example of the ecological process of primary succession. It has superlative scenery and is the habitat of threatened rufous-throated solitaire, broad-winged hawk, Martinique trembler, Martinique white-breasted thrasher, and the snake *Dromicus cursor*.

Criteria: (ii), (iii)

25. **Name of property**: DARIEN NATIONAL PARK (elected WHS 1981)

Country: Panama

Universal significance: The Darien National Park, an area of about 575,000 ha, presents the best prospect in Central America for conserving the great diversity of ecosystems, habitats, and species characteristic of this tropical rainforest environment. Habitats range from sandy beaches to upland moist tropical forest, supporting threatened species such as bush dog, jaguar, ocelot, Baird's tapir, harpy eagle, Central American caiman, and American crocodile. The Park is sufficiently large to ensure the continuation of evolutionary processes and the survival of the endangered species contained therein. The Park Master Plan is very modern in its approach to integral and rational management of a large wildland area for the benefit of local people.

Criteria: (ii), (iii), (iv).

26. **Name of property**: DEFENSORES DE CHACO NATIONAL PARK

Country: Paraguay

Universal significance: This area of 780,000 ha is the finest example of the dry chaco woodland and its associated fauna. The wild nature of the area is indicated by the fact that the latest species of large mammal to be discovered, the Chaco Peccary, was discovered in the site as recently as 1974 (having been known previously only from Pleistocene fossil deposits). The site also supports healthy populations of many other important species, including jaguar, puma, ocelot, maned wolf, and several species of armadillo.

Criteria: (ii), (iii), (iv)

27. **Name of property**: MANU NATIONAL PARK

Country: Peru

Universal significance: Manu, covering 1,532,806 ha, is situated in the upper basin of Rio Manu, ranging from 200 metres to over 4,000 metres elevation; vegetation extends from tropical rainforest to paramo grasslands. The fauna is extremely rich, with a fascinating contrast between new elements which have moved in from the north (bears, deer) and the ancient

The Vicuna is an endangered species found only in the high Andes from Chile to Peru. (Photo: WWF)

66

Macchu Picchu National Sanctuary, Peru. (Photo: Hartmut Jungius, WWF)

forms which have evolved in South America (anteaters, sloths, armadillos); the high number of primate species reflects a rich ecosystem with diverse types of forest vegetation. Threatened species include the red uakari, giant otter, jaguar, black caiman, and ocelot. The area is inhabited only by small groups of Machiguenga, Yaminahua, and Amahuaca Indians; there are also numerous archaeological sites.

Criteria: (i), (ii), (iii), (iv), plus cultural criteria.

28. **Name of property**: MACCHU PICCHU NATIONAL SANCTUARY

Country: Peru

Universal significance: Macchu Picchu covers 32,500 ha in some of the scenically most attractive mountainous territory of the Peruvian Andes. As the last stronghold of the Incas and of superb architectural and archaeological importance, Macchu Picchu is one of the most important cultural sites in Latin America. It also contains a number of endemic species.

Criteria: (ii), (iii), plus cultural criteria (dominant).

29. **Name of property**: EVERGLADES NATIONAL PARK (Florida); (elected WH Site 1979)

Country: USA

Universal significance: Everglades National Park covers an area of over 566,000 ha, protecting what is North America's premier swampy habitat. It includes significant swampy areas, both fresh water and brackish water; although surrounding irrigation and water control projects have had an impact on the Everglades, the water regime is still sufficient to support extraordinary numbers of wildlife, including endangered species such as the Florida cougar, bald eagle, brown pelican, the American crocodile, manatee, and the roseate spoon-bill. The site is also recognized as a Biosphere Reserve.

Criteria: (i), (ii), (iii), (iv).

30. **Name of property**: ANGEL FALLS AND AUYAN-TEPUY

Country: Venezuela

Universal significance: Discovered only in 1935, Angel Falls are the world's highest (c. 1,000 metres), falling from the top of the Gran Sabana (Great Plain) to the deeply-incised surrounding valley; many other falls in the 100,000 ha site are nearly as spectacular. The area is within the 3,000,000 ha Canaima National Park, which should perhaps be the property nominated.

Criteria: (iii)

31. **Name of property**: CUEVA DEL GUACHARO NATIONAL PARK

Country: Venezuela

Universal significance: This small site of 15,500 ha contains caves which are the best habitat of a bird which is so unique that it is placed in a family of its own: the Guacharo or Oilbird *(Steatornis caripensis*: Steatornithidae). The birds roost in the caves during the day, often being found in pitch darkness; experiments have shown that they find their way in the dark by using sonar. The area is also scenically attractive and contains several endemic species.

Criteria: (ii), (iii), (iv)

32. **Name of property**: JAUA-SARISARINAMA NATIONAL PARK

Country: Venezuela

Universal significance: Covering 330,000 hectares of tropical rainforest, this national park contains superb examples of unique geological formations called "tepuyes", high plateaux standing 2-3,000m above the forest, which contain very high numbers of endemic species.

Criteria: (iii), (iv)

33. **Name of property**: HENRY PITTIER NATIONAL PARK

Country: Venezuela

Universal significance: Covering 107,800 hectares, this site covers an incredible range of biotopes, from the Caribbean coast over the coastal mountain range and down the other side almost to Valencia Lake. The fauna is particularly rich, with over 530 species of birds (30 of hummingbirds alone) and an insect fauna containing two species which are the largest of their families: the mariposa *Tiramica agriprina* and the scarab *Megasoma gigas*. One of the most spectacular and unique phenomena in this national park is the spring and autumn migrations of millions of birds and butterflies, at Portachuelo.

Criteria: (iv)

Swamp forest in Everglades National Park, USA. (Photo: O. Kraus, WWF)

ACKNOWLEDGEMENTS

This paper is a joint effort of a number of people within CNPPA and from outside. The list was first proposed in 1979 by Harold Eidsvik, then Executive Officer of CNPPA. Important contributions were made by:

Lyn de Alwis
Abelardo Vildoso Baca
Maria Buchinger
Cecilia de Blohm
F. William Burley
Robert Cahn
Chao Ching Ju
Kai-Curry Lindahl
Jared Diamond
Ray Dasmann
Bernd von Droste

Harold Eidsvik
Jose Garcia
Julie Gardner
Ian Grimwood
Jeremy Harrison
Eulogio Herrera
Ivor Jackson
Peter Jackson
Maria T. Jorge Padua
Ricardo Luti

Craig MacFarland
Michael McCloskey
Kenton Miller
Robert Milne
Roger Morales
J.G. Mosley
Norman Myers
Juan Oltremari
Cesar Ormazabal
Oscar Pollard
Duncan Poore

Allen Putney
Manuel Rios
Mauricio Rosenfeld
Pedro Salinas
Heliodoro Sanchez
Hugh Synge
Tom Thomas
James Thorsell
Hernan Torres
Gary Wetterberg

The list has been compiled and edited by Jeffrey A. McNeely, the Executive Officer of CNPPA.

ANNEX I. CONVENTION FOR THE PROTECTION OF THE WORLD CULTURAL AND NATURAL HERITAGE

List of States having deposited an instrument of ratification or acceptance as at 1 September 1982

AFGHANISTAN
ALGERIA
ARGENTINA
AUSTRALIA
BENIN
BOLIVIA
BRAZIL
BULGARIA
BURUNDI
CANADA
CENTRAL AFRICAN REPUBLIC
CHILE
COSTA RICA
CUBA
CYPRUS
DEMOCRATIC YEMEN
DENMARK
ECUADOR
EGYPT
ETHIOPIA
FRANCE
GERMANY (Federal Republic of)
GHANA

GREECE
GUATEMALA
GUINEA
GUYANA
HAITI
HONDURAS
INDIA
IRAN
IRAQ
ITALY
IVORY COAST
JORDAN
LIBYAN ARAB JAMAHIRIYA
MALAWI
MALI
MALTA
MAURITANIA
MAURITIUS
MONACO
MOROCCO
NEPAL

NICARAGUA
NIGER
NIGERIA
NORWAY
OMAN
PAKISTAN
PANAMA
PERU
POLAND
PORTUGAL
SAUDI ARABIA
SENEGAL
SEYCHELLES
SPAIN
SRI LANKA
SUDAN
SWITZERLAND
SYRIAN ARAB REPUBLIC
TUNISIA
UNITED REPUBLIC OF TANZANIA
UNITED STATES OF AMERICA
YUGOSLAVIA
ZAIRE

African elephant. (Photo : Norman Myers)